EARLY NETHERLANDISH PAINTING

ITS ORIGINS AND CHARACTER

The Charles Eliot Norton Lectures
1947-1948

EARLY NETHERLANDISH PAINTING

ITS ORIGINS AND CHARACTER

BY

Erwin Panofsky

VOLUME TWO

Icon Editions
Harper & Row, Publishers
New York, Evanston, San Francisco, London

This book was originally published by Harvard University Press. First Icon edition published 1971.

STANDARD BOOK NUMBER: 06—436683-9

LIBRARY OF CONGRESS CATALOG CARD NUMBER: 52-5402

LIST OF ILLUSTRATIONS IN VOLUME TWO

Figure

1. New York, Morgan Library: Ms. 729 (Psalter of Yolande de Soissons), fol. 345 v. The Crucifixion.

2. Paris, Bibliothèque Nationale: Ms. lat. 1023 (Breviary of Philip the Fair), fol. 7 v. The Anointing of David; David's Victory over Goliath.

3. Paris, Bibliothèque Nationale: Ms. lat. 8504 (The Book of Kalila and Dimna), fol. 1 v. Philip the Fair and His Family.

4. Paris, Bibliothèque de l'Arsenal: Ms. 5059 (Bible of Jean de Papeleu), fol. 191. Job, His Wife and One of His Friends.

5. Paris, Rothschild Collection: Hours of Jeanne d'Evreux, fol. 16. The Annunciation.

6. Duccio di Buoninsegna: The Annunciation of the Virgin's Death. Siena, Opera del Duomo.

7. Paris, Rothschild Collection: Hours of Jeanne d'Evreux, fol. 82 v. The Lamentation.

8. Duccio di Buoninsegna: The Lamentation. Siena, Opera del Duomo.

9. Verdun, Bibliothèque Municipale: Ms. 107 (Breviary of Marguérite de Bar), fol. 12; In the Initial, The Anointing of David.

10. Paris, Bibliothèque Nationale: Ms. lat. 10483 (Belleville Breviary), fol. 24 v; In the Initial, Saul Casting the Javelin at David.

11. Paris, Bibliothèque Nationale: Ms. lat. 10483 (Belleville Breviary), fol. 6 v. December.

12. Paris, Bibliothèque Nationale: Ms. lat. 10484 (Belleville Breviary), fol. 2. January.

13. London, British Museum: Paris, Rothschild Collection (Hours of Jeanne II de Navarre), fol. 4 v. February.

14. London, British Museum: Paris, Rothschild Collection (Hours of Jeanne II de Navarre), fol. 5. March.

15. Formerly Florence, Baron H. de Landau (Present Whereabouts Unknown): Hours of Bonne of Luxembourg, fol. 2 v. February.

16. Paris, Bibliothèque Nationale: Ms. lat. 18014 (*Petites Heures*), fol. 2. March.

17. Paris, Bibliothèque Nationale: Ms. fr. 1950 (*Information des Princes*), fol. 2. Presentation of the Volume to Charles V.

18. Portsmouth, England, Catholic Episcopal Library: *Heures de Savoie*, fol. 2. Blanche of Burgundy Adoring the Trinity.

19. Portsmouth, England, Catholic Episcopal Library: *Heures de Savoie*, fol. 4 v. St. Leonard.

20. The Hague, Museum Meermanno-Westreenianum: Ms. 10 B 23 (Bible of Charles V, Dated 1371), fol. 513 v. Christ Healing the Palsied Man.

21. The Hague, Museum Meermanno-Westreenianum: Ms. 10 B 23 (Bible of Charles V, Dated 1371), fol. 134 v. David's Victory over Goliath.

22. The Hague, Museum Meermanno-Westreenianum: Ms. 10 A 14 (Ghent Missal, Dated 1366), fol. 22. The Nativity.

23. The Hague, Museum Meermanno-Westreenianum: Ms. 10 B 23 (Bible of Charles V, Dated 1371), fols. 1 v., 2. Inscription of Jean Bondol; Presentation of the Volume to Charles V by Jean de Vaudetar.

24. Paris, Bibliothèque Nationale: Ms. fr. 15397 (Bible of Jean de Sy), fol. 36. Lot and His Daughters.

ILLUSTRATIONS

25. Angers, Musée des Tapisseries: The Dead Which Die in the Lord (Tapestry from the Series Known as the "Angers Apocalypse"; Revelation XIV, 13).

26. Paris, Bibliothèque Nationale: Ms. fr. 13091 (Psalter of the Duc de Berry), fol. 9 v. David.

27. Paris, Bibliothèque Nationale: Ms. fr. 13091 (Psalter of the Duc de Berry), fol. 24. St. John the Evangelist.

28. Paris, Louvre: Portrait of Jean le Bon.

29. Paris, Louvre: Calvary and Donors (Charles V and Jeanne de Bourbon), Central Section of the *Parement de Narbonne* (Grisaille Painting on Silk).

30. Paris, Bibliothèque Nationale: Ms. lat. 18014 (*Petites Heures*), fol. 22. The Annunciation; The Man of Sorrows between the Madonna and St. John the Baptist; The Apostles; Jeremiah.

31. Paris, Bibliothèque Nationale: Ms. lat. 18014 (*Petites Heures*), fol. 209 v. The Baptism of Christ.

32. Paris, Bibliothèque Nationale: Ms. lat. 18014 (*Petites Heures*), fol. 141 v. The Annunciation.

33. Paris, Bibliothèque Nationale: Ms. lat. 18014 (*Petites Heures*), fol. 208. St. John the Baptist in the Wilderness.

34. Paris, Bibliothèque Nationale: Ms. lat. 18014 (*Petites Heures*), fol. 94 v. The Lamentation.

35. Paris, Bibliothèque Nationale: Ms. lat. 18014 (*Petites Heures*), fol. 286. The Lamentation.

36. Paris, Bibliothèque Nationale: Ms. lat. 18014 (*Petites Heures*), fol. 82. The Derision of Christ.

37. Turin, Museo Civico (Formerly Milan, Principe Trivulzio): *Les Très-Belles Heures de Notre Dame*, fol. 4 v. The Nativity. Copyright ACL, Bruxelles.

38. Pisan Master of the Early Fifteenth Century (Formerly Called Vanni Falcone): The Nativity. Pisa, Museo Civico.

39. Paris, Rothschild Collection: *Les Très-Belles Heures de Notre Dame*, fol. 216. The Descent from the Cross.

40. Brussels, Bibliothèque Royale: Ms. 11060/61 ("Brussels Hours"), fols. 10 v. and 11. The Duc de Berry Presented to the Madonna by St. John the Baptist and St. Andrew.

41. Brussels, Bibliothèque Royale: Ms. 11060/61 ("Brussels Hours"), fol. 14. The Duc de Berry Presented to the Madonna by St. John the Baptist and St. Andrew.

42. Brussels, Bibliothèque Royale: Ms. 11060/61 ("Brussels Hours"), fol. 18. The Annunciation.

43. Brussels, Bibliothèque Royale: Ms. 11060/61 ("Brussels Hours"), fol. 54. The Visitation.

44. Brussels, Bibliothèque Royale: Ms. 11060/61 ("Brussels Hours"), fol. 106. The Flight into Egypt.

45. Brussels, Bibliothèque Royale: Ms. 11060/61 ("Brussels Hours"), fol. 186. The Bearing of the Cross.

46. Simone Martini: The Bearing of the Cross. Paris, Louvre.

47. Paris, Bibliothèque Nationale: Ms. lat. 919 (*Grandes Heures*), fol. 77; In the Initial, The Lamentation.

48. Paris, Bibliothèque Nationale: Ms. lat. 919 (*Grandes Heures*), fol. 100. St. Gregory.

49. Paris, Bibliothèque Nationale: Ms. lat. 919 (*Grandes Heures*), fol. 96. The Duc de Berry Welcomed by St. Peter at the Gates of Paradise.

50. Paris, Bibliothèque Nationale: Ms. fr. 616 (Gaston Phébus, *Livre de Chasse*), fol. 50. The Bird Hound and His Whole Nature.

ILLUSTRATIONS

51. Paris, Bibliothèque Nationale: Ms. fr. 12201 (*Fleur des Histoires de la Terre d'Orient*), fol. 17 v. The Land of the Tartars.

52. Brussels, Bibliothèque Royale: Ms. 9125 (Missal of the Sainte-Chapelle), fol. 177 v. The Crucifixion.

53. Paris, Bibliothèque Nationale: Ms. fr. 598 (*Boccace du Duc de Berry*), fol. 46. Penthesilea.

54. Paris, Bibliothèque Nationale: Ms. fr. 12420 (*Boccace de Philippe le Hardi*), fol. 29. Antiope and Oreithyia.

55. Paris, Bibliothèque Nationale: Ms. fr. 598 (*Boccace du Duc de Berry*), fol. 71 v. Sappho.

56. Paris, Bibliothèque Nationale: Ms. fr. 598 (*Boccace du Duc de Berry*), fol. 99. Cimon and Pero (*Caritas Romana*).

57. Paris, Bibliothèque de l'Arsenal: Ms. 5057 (*Bible Historiale*), fol. 7. The Creation of Adam.

58. Paris, Bibliothèque de l'Arsenal: Ms. 5058 (*Bible Historiale*), fol. 1. The Judgment and Parables of Solomon.

59. Paris, Musée Jacquemart-André: The Hours of the Maréchal de Boucicaut, fol. 65 v. The Visitation.

60. Paris, Musée Jacquemart-André: The Hours of the Maréchal de Boucicaut, fol. 53 v. The Annunciation.

61. Paris, Musée Jacquemart-André: The Hours of the Maréchal de Boucicaut, fol. 171 v. St. Jerome.

62. Paris, Musée Jacquemart-André: The Hours of the Maréchal de Boucicaut, fol. 142 v. The Vigils of the Dead.

63. Paris, Musée Jacquemart-André: The Hours of the Maréchal de Boucicaut, fol. 95 v. The Coronation of the Virgin.

64. Paris, Musée Jacquemart-André: The Hours of the Maréchal de Boucicaut, fol. 26 v. The Maréchal de Boucicaut and His Wife, Antoinette de Turenne, Venerating the Madonna.

65. Paris, Musée Jacquemart-André: The Hours of the Maréchal de Boucicaut, fol. 38 v. The Maréchal de Boucicaut Venerating St. Catherine.

66. Paris, Musée Jacquemart-André: The Hours of the Maréchal de Boucicaut, fol. 73 v. The Nativity.

67. Paris, Musée Jacquemart-André: The Hours of the Maréchal de Boucicaut, fol. 83 v. The Adoration of the Magi.

68. Paris, Bibliothèque Nationale: Ms. fr. 23279 (*Dialogues de Pierre Salmon*), fol. 69. The Author Presenting One of His Letters to Charles VI and Delivering, in the Latter's Name, a Cope and Chalice to Notre-Dame-de-Hal in Brabant.

69. Geneva, Bibliothèque Publique et Universitaire: Ms. fr. 165 (*Dialogues de Pierre Salmon*), fol. 4. Charles VI with His Retinue and the Author.

70. Paris, Bibliothèque Nationale: Ms. lat. 10538 (Book of Hours), fol. 137 v. The Vigils of the Dead.

71. Bourges, Bibliothèque de la Ville: Ms. 34 (Lectionary of the Duc de Berry), fol. 46 v. The Birth of St. John.

72. Paris, Bibliothèque Nationale: Ms. lat. 10538 (Book of Hours), fol. 63. The Nativity.

73. Baltimore, Walters Art Gallery: Ms. 260 (Book of Hours), fol. 63 v. The Nativity.

74. Paris, Bibliothèque Nationale: Ms. lat. 1161 (Book of Hours), fol. 31. The Annunciation.

75. Paris, Bibliothèque Nationale: Ms. lat. 1161 (Book of Hours), fol. 27. The *Pieté Nostre Seigneur*.

76. Paris, Bibliothèque Nationale: Ms. lat. 1161 (Book of Hours), fol. 212. Funeral Service in the Cemetery.

ILLUSTRATIONS

77. Paris, Bibliothèque Nationale: Ms. fr. 2810 (*Livre des Merveilles du Monde*), fol. 11 v. The Three Magi on Their Journey Through Persia, Detail.

78. Paris, Bibliothèque Nationale: Ms. lat. 1161 (Book of Hours), fol. 290. The Owner Venerating the Madonna.

79. Paris, Bibliothèque Nationale: Ms. fr. 259 (*Tite-Live*), fol. 253. The Coronation of Hannibal.

80. Chantilly, Musée Condé: *Les Très Riches Heures du Duc de Berry*, fol. 26. The Annunciation.

81. Chantilly, Musée Condé: *Les Très Riches Heures du Duc de Berry*, fol. 44 v. The Nativity and Annunciation to the Shepherds.

82. Chantilly, Musée Condé: *Les Très Riches Heures du Duc de Berry*, fol. 25. The Fall of Man and the Expulsion from Paradise.

83. Chantilly, Musée Condé: *Les Très Riches Heures du Duc de Berry*, fol. 17. St. John the Evangelist on Patmos.

84. Chantilly, Musée Condé: *Les Très Riches Heures du Duc de Berry*, fol. 51 v. The Meeting of the Three Magi at the Crossroads near Bethlehem.

85. The Emperor Constantine: Medal of the Duc de Berry. Vienna, Kunsthistorisches Museum.

86. Giotto, The Stigmatization of St. Francis. Florence, Santa Croce.

87. Chantilly, Musée Condé: *Les Très Riches Heures du Duc de Berry*, fol. 142 v. Christ at Gethsemane.

88. Chantilly, Musée Condé: *Les Très Riches Heures du Duc de Berry*, fol. 1 v. January.

89. Chantilly, Musée Condé: *Les Très Riches Heures du Duc de Berry*, fol. 2 v. February.

90. Chantilly, Musée Condé: *Les Très Riches Heures du Duc de Berry*, fol. 3 v. March.

91. Chantilly, Musée Condé: *Les Très Riches Heures du Duc de Berry*, fol. 4 v. April.

92. Franco-Flemish Master of *ca.* 1420: Portrait of a Young Lady. Washington, National Gallery of Art (Mellon Collection). *Courtesy of the National Gallery of Art, Washington.*

93. Chantilly, Musée Condé: *Les Très Riches Heures du Duc de Berry*, fol. 52. Detail of the "Adoration of the Magi."

94. Copy after the April Master of the *Très Riches Heures du Duc de Berry*: Portrait of John the Fearless. Paris, Louvre.

95. Chantilly, Musée Condé: *Les Très Riches Heures du Duc de Berry*, Detail of fig. 91.

96. Cambridge, Massachusetts, Harvard University Library: The De Buz Hours, fol. 155. Madonna Standing.

97. Paris, Bibliothèque Nationale: Ms. lat. 9471 (*Grandes Heures de la Famille de Rohan*), fol. 85 v. The Annunciation to the Shepherds.

98. Paris, Bibliothèque Nationale: Ms. lat. 9471 (*Grandes Heures de la Famille de Rohan*), fol. 135. The Dying Man Commending His Soul to God.

99. Valencian Master of 1420–1425: Madonna and Saints; Calvary ("Carrand Diptych"). Florence, Museo Nazionale.

100. Jean Malouel and Henri Bellechose: The Martyrdom of St. Denis and His Companions. Paris, Louvre.

101. Jean Malouel: The Trinity with the Virgin Mary and St. John the Evangelist. Paris, Louvre.

102. French Master of *ca.* 1410: The Coronation of the Virgin. Berlin, Kaiser Friedrich Museum.

103. Utrecht Master of 1363: The Calvary of Hendrik van Rijn. Antwerp, Musée Royal des Beaux-Arts.

ILLUSTRATIONS

104. Melchior Broederlam: The Annunciation; The Visitation (Companion Piece of fig. 105). Dijon, Musée de la Ville.

105. Melchior Broederlam: The Presentation of Christ; The Flight into Egypt (Companion Piece of fig. 104). Dijon, Musée de la Ville.

106. Mosan Master of *ca.* 1415: Exterior of a Triptych (see fig. 107). The Annunciation; The Adoration of the Magi; Two Groups of Saints. Vierhouten, D. G. van Beuningen Collection.

107. Mosan Master of *ca.* 1415: Interior of a Triptych (see fig. 106). The Coronation of the Virgin; The *Piété Nostre Seigneur*: Four Groups of Saints; St. Stephen; St. Lawrence. Vierhouten, D. G. van Beuningen Collection.

108. Guelders (?) Master of 1400–1410: Left Half of a Quadriptych (see fig. 109). *a*. The Baptism of Christ (Exterior), Baltimore, Walters Art Gallery; *b*. The Annunciation, Baltimore, Walters Art Gallery; *c*. The Nativity, Antwerp, Mayer van den Bergh Collection. *Courtesy of the Walters Art Gallery, Baltimore.*

109. Guelders (?) Master of *ca.* 1400–1410: Right Half of a Quadriptych (see fig. 108). *a*. St. Christopher (Exterior), Antwerp, Mayer van den Bergh Collection; *b*. The Crucifixion, Baltimore, Walters Art Gallery; *c*. The Resurrection, Antwerp, Mayer van den Bergh Collection. *Courtesy of the Walters Art Gallery, Baltimore.*

110. North Guelders or Cleves (?) Master of 1410–1415: The Nativity. Berlin, Deutsches Museum.

111. Follower of Melchior Broederlam: Quadriptych. The Nativity; The Presentation of Christ; The Adoration of the Magi; The Massacre of the Innocents; The Flight into Egypt. Antwerp, Mayer van den Bergh Collection.

112. Brabantine Master of *ca.* 1400: The Birth of the Virgin, Detail from a Life of the Virgin. Brussels, Musée Royal.

113. Bruges Master of *ca.* 1400: The Calvary of the Tanners. Bruges, St.-Sauveur.

114. Brussels, Bibliothèque Royale: Ms. 205 A (Bible of Hendrik van Arnheim), fol. 1. Alexander the Great Dividing His Realm on His Deathbed.

115. Baltimore, Walters Art Gallery: Ms. 171 (Dirc van Delft, *Tafel van den Kersten Ghelove*), fol. 5 v. The Creation of the World.

116. New York, Morgan Library: Ms. 691 (Dirc van Delft, *Tafel van den Kersten Ghelove*), fol. 119. Emperor, Knight and Husbandman.

117. London, British Museum: Ms. Add. 22288 (Dirc van Delft, *Tafel van den Kersten Ghelove*), fol. 180. Christ in the Winepress.

118. Baltimore, Walters Art Gallery: Ms. 185 (Book of Hours), fol. 137 v. The Last Judgment.

119. London, British Museum: Ms. Add. 38527 (*Spieghel der Maeghden*), fol. 90 v. The Madonna Enthroned.

120. Berlin, Staatsbibliothek: Cod. germ. 4° 42 (Prayer Book of Mary of Guelders, Dated 1415), fols. 19 v., 20. The Duchess of Guelders in the Garden Inclosed; The Betrayal of Christ.

121. New York, Morgan Library: Ms. 87 (Breviary of Renaud IV of Guelders), fol. 428; in the Initial, The *Salvator Mundi*.

122. New York, Morgan Library: Ms. 87 (Breviary of Renaud IV of Guelders), fol. 260 v.; in the Initial, David's Victory over Goliath.

123. New York, Morgan Library: Ms. 87 (Breviary of Renaud IV of Guelders), fol. 387 v. The Brazen Serpent.

124. New York, Morgan Library: Ms. 87 (Breviary of Renaud IV of Guelders), fol. 81 v. St. John the Baptist Preaching.

125. New York, Morgan Library: Ms. 87 (Breviary of Renaud IV of Guelders), fol. 291 v. The Prophet Jonah.

126. New York, Morgan Library: Ms. 87 (Breviary of Renaud IV of Guelders), fol. 404 v. The Coronation of the Virgin.

ILLUSTRATIONS

127. Formerly Kottbus, Dr. Alfred Bum Collection: Book of Hours, fol. 28 v. The Nativity.

128. The Hague, Museum Meermanno-Westreenianum: Ms. 10 E 1 (Book of Hours, Dated 1438), fol. 77 v. The Adoration of the Magi.

129. Nordkirchen, Duke of Arenberg Collection: Hours of Catherine of Cleves (not foliated). The Crucifixion.

130. Nordkirchen, Duke of Arenberg Collection: Hours of Catherine of Cleves (not foliated). The Descent from the Cross.

131. Liége, Bibliothèque Universitaire: Ms. 35 (Book of Hours), fol. 17 v. The Annunciation.

132. Liége, Bibliothèque Universitaire: Ms. 35 (Book of Hours), fol. 49 v. The Nativity.

133. London, British Museum: Ms. Egerton 859 (Prayer Book, perhaps of Mary of Cleves), fol. 30. Chorus of Angels.

134. London, British Museum: Ms. Egerton 859 (Prayer Book, perhaps of Mary of Cleves), fol. 31. Susanna and the Elders.

135. New York, Morgan Library: Ms. 785 (Abû Ma'šar's *Liber Astrologiae*, fraudulently claimed by Georgius Zothori Zapari Fenduli), fol. 34. Saturn in His Mansions (Capricorn and Aquarius).

136. New York, Morgan Library: Ms. 785 (Abû Ma'šar's *Liber Astrologiae*, fraudulently claimed by Georgius Zothori Zapari Fenduli), fol. 48. Mercury in Exaltation (in the Sign of the Virgin).

137. New York, Morgan Library: Ms. 785 (Abû Ma'šar *Liber Astrologiae*, fraudulently claimed by Georgius Zothori Zapari Fenduli), fol. 50. The Moon in Exaltation (in the Sign of the Bull).

138. Brussels, Bibliothèque Royale: Ms. 10176/78 (Guillaume de Deguileville, *Pèlerinages*), fol. 78. The Pilgrim, Envy, Treason, and Detraction.

139. Wiesbaden, Staatsarchiv: Miscellaneous Manuscript, Dated 1410. Five Jews Attempting to Stone the Lord.

140. Brussels, Bibliothèque Royale: Ms. 11041 (Laurent Du Bois, *Somme-le-Roy*, Dated 1415), fol. 81 v. Equity, Felony, Noah's Ark, and Moses Enforcing Peace.

141. Brussels, Bibliothèque Royale: Ms. 11041 (Laurent Du Bois, *Somme-le-Roy*, Dated 1415), fol. 52 v. The Sermon on the Mount.

142. Brussels, Bibliothèque Royale (Formerly Brussels, Beaulieu de Colbert Collection): Ms. II, 7831 (*Les Examples Moraux*, Known as *Ci nous dist*), fol. 21. The Annunciation.

143. Brussels, Bibliothèque Royale (Formerly Brussels, Beaulieu de Colbert Collection): Ms. II, 7831 (*Les Examples Moraux*, Known as *Ci nous dist*), fol. 22. The Nativity.

144. Brussels, Bibliothèque Royale (Formerly Brussels, Beaulieu de Colbert Collection): Ms. II, 7831 (*Les Examples Moraux*, Known as *Ci nous dist*), fol. 25 v. The Entry into Jerusalem.

145. Paris, Bibliothèque Nationale: Ms. lat. 1364 (Book of Hours), fol. 25. The Annunciation.

146. Paris Bibliothèque Nationale: Ms. lat. 1364 (Book of Hours), fol. 37 v. The Baptism of Christ.

147. Brussels, Bibliothèque Royale (Formerly Brussels, Beaulieu de Colbert Collection): Ms. II, 7831 (*Les Examples Moraux*, Known as *Ci nous dist*), fol. 27. The Last Supper.

148. Brussels, Bibliothèque Royale (Formerly Brussels, Beaulieu de Colbert Collection): Ms. II, 7831 (*Les Examples Moraux*, Known as *Ci nous dist*), fol. 44. Christ Appearing to His Mother.

149. Tournai, Bibliothèque Municipale: Ms. 42 (*Riegle et Ordenance des Soers del Hostelerie Nostre Dame de Tournay*), fol. 1. Three Leading Ladies of the Society Venerating the Madonna.

ILLUSTRATIONS

150. Paris, Bibliothèque Nationale: Ms. néerl. 3 (*Apocalipsis in Dietsche*), fol. 2. Revelation. Chapter I.

151. Paris, Bibliothèque Nationale: Ms. néerl. 3 (*Apocalipsis in Dietsche*), fol. 3. Revelation, Chapters II, III.

152. Paris, Bibliothèque Nationale: Ms. néerl. 3 (*Apocalipsis in Dietsche*), fol. 9. Revelation, Chapter VIII.

153. Liége (?) Master of ca. 1400: Triptych. The Trinity Surrounded by the Evangelists. Berlin, Deutsches Museum.

154. Rouen, Bibliothèque de la Ville: Ms. 3024 (Book of Hours), fol. 12 v. The Owner Presented to the Madonna by St. George.

155. Rouen, Bibliothèque de la Ville: Ms. 3024 (Book of Hours), fol. 53 v. The Flight into Egypt.

156. Rouen, Bibliothèque de la Ville: Ms. 3024 (Book of Hours), fol. 13. The Annunciation.

157. Rouen, Bibliothèque de la Ville: Ms. 3024 (Book of Hours), fol. 40 v. The Nativity.

158. Rouen, Bibliothèque de la Ville: Ms. 3024 (Book of Hours), fol. 94 v. The Holy Face.

159. Carpentras, Bibliothèque de la Ville: Ms. 57 (Book of Hours), fol. 55 v. The Madonna, St. Catherine and St. Agnes in the Garden of Paradise.

160. Frankfort, Museum für Kunsthandwerk: Ms. Linel 11 (Miniature Inserted in a Book of Hours). The Owner Venerating St. Bernard.

161. Frankfort, Museum für Kunsthandwerk: Ms. Linel 11 (Miniature Inserted in a Book of Hours). The Annunciation.

162. Oxford, Bodleian Library: Ms. Canonici Liturg. 118 (19263; Book of Hours), fol. 19 v. St. Christopher.

163. Carpentras, Bibliothèque de la Ville: Ms. 57 (Book of Hours), fol. 65 v. St. Christopher.

164. Melchior Broederlam: Prophet Statue, Detail from fig. 104.

165. Indianapolis, Dr. G. H. A. Clowes Collection: Book of Hours, fol. 42 v. The Annunciation. *Courtesy of Dr. G. H. A. Clowes.*

166. London, British Museum: Ms. Add. 29704 (Cuttings from a Carmelite Missal), fol. 35. The Immaculate Conception.

167. London, British Museum. Ms. Add. 29704 (Cuttings from a Carmelite Missal), fol. 83. St. Louis.

168. London, British Museum: Ms. 16998 (Book of Hours), fol. 37. St. John the Evangelist.

169. London, British Museum: Ms. Add. 29704 (Cuttings from a Carmelite Missal), fol. 14. The Investiture of St. Martin; St. Martin and the Beggar.

170. London, British Museum: Ms. Add. 16998 (Book of Hours), fol. 17. The Annunciation.

171. London, British Museum. Ms. Add. 16998 (Book of Hours), fol. 67. Portrait of the Owner.

172. London, British Museum: Ms. Add. 16998 (Book of Hours), fol. 65. The Madonna of Humility.

173. London, British Museum: Ms. Royal 2 A XVIII (Beaufort Hours), fol. 11 v. St. Christopher.

174. London, British Museum: Ms. Royal 2 A XVIII (Beaufort Hours), fol. 23 v. The Annunciation with the Owners, probably John de Beaufort and Margaret of Holland.

175. London, Lambeth Palace, Library: Ms. 69 (Chichele Breviary), fol. 4 v. The Annunciation. *Reproduced with permission of the Archbishop of Canterbury and the Church Commission.*

176. London, British Museum: Ms. Add. 42131 (Bedford Psalter and Hours), fol. 7. The Annunciation.

177. London, British Museum: Ms. Add. 42131 (Bedford Psalter and Hours), fol. 73. The Anointing of David.

178. London, British Museum: Ms. Add. 42131 (Bedford Psalter and Hours), fol. 33. The Entombment.

179. London, British Museum: Ms. Add. 18213 (Book of Hours), fol. 13. The Annunciation.

180. London, British Museum: Ms. Add. 18213 (Book of Hours), fol. 34. The Nativity.

181. English Master of *ca.* 1415: The "Wilton Diptych." Richard II Presented to the Madonna by St. John the Baptist, St. Edward and St. Edmund. London, National Gallery.

182. Paris, Bibliothèque Nationale: Ms. lat. Nouv. Acq. 3055 (Hours of John the Fearless), fol. 89 v. The Nativity.

183. Paris, Bibliothèque Nationale: Ms. lat. Nouv. Acq. 3055 (Hours of John the Fearless), fol. 178 v. St. Christopher.

184. Paris, Bibliothèque Nationale: Ms. lat. Nouv. Acq. 3055 (Hours of John the Fearless), fol. 40 v. The Derision of Christ.

185. Paris, Bibliothèque Nationale: Ms. lat. Nouv. Acq. 3055 (Hours of John the Fearless), fol. 172 v. St. Andrew.

186. Baltimore, Walters Art Gallery: Ms. 166 (Hours of Daniel Rym), fol. 168 v. Daniel in the Lions' Den Venerated by Daniel Rym.

187. Baltimore, Walters Art Gallery: Ms. 166 (Hours of Daniel, Rym), fol. 160 v. St. Christopher and St. Anthony.

188. Baltimore, Walters Art Gallery: Ms. 166 (Hours of Daniel Rym), fol. 113 v. The Bearing of the Cross.

189. Baltimore, Walters Art Gallery: Ms. 166 (Hours of Daniel Rym), fol. 106 v. The Betrayal of Christ.

190. Baltimore, Walters Art Gallery: Ms. 170 (Book of Hours), fol. 172 v. St. Barbara.

191. Baltimore, Walters Art Gallery: Ms. 211 (Book of Hours), fol. 155 v. The Rest on the Flight into Egypt.

192. New York, Morgan Library: Ms. 439 (Book of Hours), fol. 21 v. St. John the Baptist.

193. Providence, John Carter Brown Library: Ms. 3 (Book of Hours, not foliated). St. George Slaying the Dragon.

194. Lisbon, National Archives, Armario dos Tratados: Duarte Hours, fol. 35 v. St. George Slaying the Dragon.

195. Bruges, Grand Séminaire: Ms. vol. 72/175 (Book of Hours), fol. 52. St. George Slaying the Dragon. Copyright ACL Bruxelles.

196. The Master of Flémalle: Triptych. The Entombment; The Resurrection; A Donor. London, Count A. Seilern Collection.

197. The Master of Flémalle: Detail of fig. 196.

198. The Master of Flémalle (?): Madonna of Humility. Berlin, Kaiser Friedrich Museum.

199. The Master of Flémalle: The Betrothal of the Virgin (Obverse of fig. 200). Madrid, Prado.

200. The Master of Flémalle: St. James the Great; St. Clare (Reverse of fig. 199). Madrid, Prado.

201. The Master of Flémalle: The Nativity. Dijon, Musée de la Ville.

202. The Master of Flémalle: Landscape, Detail of fig. 201.

203. The Master of Flémalle: Madonna in a Domestic Interior. London, National Gallery. *Reproduced by courtesy of the Trustees, the National Gallery, London.*

204. The Master of Flémalle: The "Mérode Altarpiece." The Annunciation; The

Donors (Inghelbrechts of Malines and His Wife); St. Joseph in His Workshop. Formerly Westerloo-Tongerloo, Princesse de Mérode Collection.

205. The Master of Flémalle: The Bad Thief and the Centurion (Fragment of a Triptych; cf. fig. 230). Frankfort, Städelsches Kunstinstitut.

206. The Master of Flémalle: Madonna Standing (Counterpart of fig. 208?). Frankfort, Städelsches Kunstinstitut.

207. The Master of Flémalle: The Trinity of the Broken Body (Originally Reverse of fig. 208). Frankfort, Städelsches Kunstinstitut.

208. The Master of Flémalle: St. Veronica (Originally Obverse of fig. 207; Counterpart of Fig. 206?). Frankfort, Städelsches Kunstinstitut.

209. The Master of Flémalle: Madonna in a Glory Appearing to St. Peter and St. Augustine, Venerated by an Augustinian Abbot. Aix-en-Provence, Musée Granet. *Courtesy of the Musée Granet, Aix-en-Provence.*

210. The Master of Flémalle: The Trinity of the Broken Body. Leningrad, Hermitage. *Courtesy of Mr. G. I. Olifirenko, Cultural Representative of VOKS at the USSR Embassy, Washington, D. C.*

211. The Master of Flémalle: The Madonna of the Fireplace. Leningrad, Hermitage. *Courtesy of Mr. G. I. Olifirenko, Cultural Representative of VOKS at the USSR Embassy, Washington, D. C.*

212. The Master of Flémalle: Left Wing of a Triptych. Heinrich von Werl Commended by St. John the Baptist, Dated 1438 (Counterpart of fig. 213). Madrid, Prado.

213. The Master of Flémalle: Right Wing of a Triptych. St. Barbara (Counterpart of fig. 212). Madrid, Prado.

214. The Master of Flémalle: Interior, Detail of fig. 213.

215. Roger van der Weyden: Interior, Detail of fig. 310.

216. The Master of Flémalle: The Virgin Mary Interceding with Christ. Philadelphia, Pennsylvania Museum of Art (Johnson Collection). *Courtesy of the John G. Johnson Art Collection, Philadelphia.*

217. The Master of Flémalle: Portrait of a Gentleman (Companion Piece of fig. 218). London, National Gallery. *Reproduced by courtesy of the Trustees, the National Gallery, London.*

218. The Master of Flémalle: Portrait of a Lady (Companion Piece of fig. 217). London, National Gallery. *Reproduced by courtesy of the Trustees, the National Gallery, London.*

219. The Master of Flémalle (?): Portrait of a Musician. New York, Mrs. J. Magnin Collection.

220. The Master of Flémalle: Portrait of Robert de Masmines (Copy?). Berlin, Kaiser Friedrich Museum.

221. The Master of Flémalle: Portrait of a Princess, Supposedly Mary of Savoy (Copy?). Dumbarton Oaks, Washington, D. C.

222. Copy after the Master of Flémalle: The Madonna in an Apse. New York, Metropolitan Museum.

223. Copy after the Master of Flémalle: The Adoration of the Magi. Berlin, Kaiser Friedrich Museum.

224. Copy after the Master of Flémalle: The Vengeance of Tomyris. Berlin, Kaiser Friedrich Museum.

225. Copy after the Master of Flémalle: Jaël Slaying Sisera (Pen Drawing). Braunschweig, Landesmuseum.

226. Copy after the Master of Flémalle: Madonna of Humility. Brussels, G. Müller Collection. *Copyright ACL, Bruxelles.*

227. Copy after the Master of Flémalle: The Mass of St. Gregory. New York, E. Schwarz Collection.

228. Colin de Coter (Probably after the Master of Flémalle): St. Luke Painting the Virgin. Vieure near Moulins, Church.

229. Gerard David (after the Master of Flémalle): The Crucifixion. Lugano, Thyssen Collection.

230. Copy after the Master of Flémalle: Triptych. *a.* St. John the Baptist and St. Julian (Exterior); *b.* The Descent from the Cross (Interior). Liverpool, Walker Art Gallery.

231. Copy after the Master of Flémalle: The Madonna Enthroned with St. Roger (?), St. Catherine and Donors (Pen Drawing). Paris, Louvre.

232. Jacques Daret: The Visitation and the Donor (Jean Du Clercq, Abbot of St. Vaast at Arras). Berlin, Kaiser Friedrich Museum.

233. Jacques Daret: The Nativity. Lugano, Thyssen Collection.

234. Jacques Daret: The Adoration of the Magi. Berlin, Kaiser Friedrich Museum.

235. Jacques Daret: The Presentation of Christ. Paris, Petit Palais.

236. Jan van Eyck: The Madonna in a Church. Berlin, Kaiser Friedrich Museum.

237. Jan van Eyck: Detail of fig. 236.

238. Jan van Eyck: The Annunciation. Washington, National Gallery of Art (Mellon Collection). *Courtesy of the National Gallery of Art, Washington.*

239. Jan van Eyck. Detail of fig. 238. *Courtesy of the National Gallery of Art, Washington.*

240. Jan van Eyck: Triptych. St. Michael and the Donor (Michele Giustiniani?); The Madonna Enthroned; St. Catherine. Dresden, Gemäldegalerie.

241. Jan van Eyck: The Madonna Enthroned, Central Panel of the Triptych, fig. 240.

242. Jan van Eyck: The Annunciation, Exterior Wings of the Triptych, fig. 240.

243. Jan van Eyck: The Madonna Enthroned, Dated 1433. Melbourne, National Gallery.

244. Jan van Eyck: The Madonna Enthroned, Venerated by Chancellor Nicholas Rolin. Paris, Louvre. *Copyright ACL Bruxelles.*

245. Jan van Eyck: Chancellor Nicholas Rolin, Detail of fig. 244.

246. Jan van Eyck: Madonna and Child, Detail of fig. 244.

247. Jan van Eyck: Portrait of Giovanni Arnolfini and Jeanne Cenami, Dated 1434. London, National Gallery. *Reproduced by courtesy of the Trustees, the National Gallery, London.*

248. Jan van Eyck: The Madonna Enthroned with St. Donatian and St. George, Venerated by Canon George van der Paele, Dated 1436. Bruges, Musée Communal. *Copyright ACL Bruxelles.*

249. Jan van Eyck: Hand of St. George, Detail of fig. 248. *Copyright ACL Bruxelles.*

250. The Master of Flémalle: Hand of the Centurion, Detail of fig. 205.

251. Roger van der Weyden: Hand of St. John the Evangelist, Detail of fig. 314.

252. Jan van Eyck: The Madonna Enthroned (The "Lucca Madonna"). Frankfort, Städelsches Kunstinstitut.

253. Jan van Eyck: The Annunciation. Lugano, Thyssen Collection.

254. Jan van Eyck: St. Barbara, Dated 1437. Antwerp, Musée Royal des Beaux-Arts. *Copyright ACL Bruxelles.*

255. Jan van Eyck: The Madonna at the Fountain, Dated 1439. Antwerp, Musée Royal des Beaux-Arts.

256. Jan van Eyck (?): The Holy Face. Durham, J. C. Swinburne Collection (?).

257. Jan van Eyck and Petrus Christus: Madonna Standing with St. Barbara and St. Elizabeth of Thuringia, Venerated by Jan Vos, Prior of the Charterhouse of Genadedal near Bruges. Paris, Robert de Rothschild Collection.

258. Jan van Eyck and Petrus Christus: St. Jerome in His Study. Detroit, Institute of Arts.

259. Commenced by Jan van Eyck: Madonna Standing, Venerated by Nicholas

van Maelbeke, Provost of St. Martin's at Ypres (Wings Later). Present Ownership Not Established.

260. Jan van Eyck: Portrait of Baudoin de Lannoy. Berlin, Kaiser Friedrich Museum.

261. Jan van Eyck: Portrait of "Timotheos" (Gilles Binchois?), Dated 1432. London, National Gallery. *Reproduced by courtesy of the Trustees, the National Gallery, London.*

262. Jan van Eyck: Portrait of a Man in a Red Turban, Dated 1433. London, National Gallery. *Reproduced by courtesy of the Trustees, the National Gallery, London.*

263. Jan van Eyck, Portrait of Nicholas Cardinal Albergati. Vienna, Gemäldegalerie.

264. Jan van Eyck, Portrait of Nicholas Cardinal Albergati (Silverpoint Drawing). Formerly Dresden, Kupferstichkabinett.

265. Jan van Eyck: Portrait of the Goldsmith Jan de Leeuw, Dated 1436. Vienna, Gemäldegalerie.

266. Jan van Eyck: Portrait of Giovanni Arnolfini. Berlin, Kaiser Friedrich Museum.

267. Jan van Eyck: Portrait of the Painter's Wife, Margaret van Eyck, Dated 1439. Bruges, Musée Communal. *Copyright ACL Bruxelles.*

268. Follower of Jan van Eyck: The Stigmatization of St. Francis. Philadelphia, Pennsylvania Museum of Art (Johnson Collection). *Courtesy of the John G. Johnson Art Collection, Philadelphia.*

269. Follower of Jan van Eyck: The Stigmatization of St. Francis. Turin, Galleria Sabauda.

270. Imitator of Jan van Eyck: Portrait of a Goldsmith. Sibiu (Rumania), Bruckenthal Museum.

271. Imitator of Jan van Eyck: The Man with the Pink. Berlin, Kaiser Friedrich Museum.

272. Pedro Nisart after Jan van Eyck: St. George Slaying the Dragon. Palma, Majorca, Museo Arqueológico.

273. Unidentified Artist: St. George Slaying the Dragon. Formerly London, Lady E. Mason Collection.

274. Jan van Eyck: The Ghent Altarpiece, Exterior. Ghent, St. Bavo's. *Copyright ACL Bruxelles.*

275. Hubert and Jan van Eyck: The Ghent Altarpiece, Interior (Present State, the Lower Left-Hand Panel Replaced by a Copy). Ghent, St. Bavo's. *Copyright ACL Bruxelles.*

276. Jan van Eyck: The Annunciation (The Ghent Altarpiece, Exterior). Ghent, St. Bavo's.

277. Jan van Eyck: Jodocus Vyd; St. John the Baptist; St. John the Evangelist; Elizabeth Borluut (The Ghent Altarpiece, Exterior). Ghent, St. Bavo's.

278. Hubert and Jan van Eyck: The Adoration of the Lamb (The Ghent Altarpiece, Interior). Ghent, St. Bavo's. *Copyright ACL Bruxelles.*

279. Hubert and Jan van Eyck: The Just Judges; The Knights of Christ; The Holy Hermits; The Holy Pilgrims (The Ghent Altarpiece, Interior). Ghent, St. Bavo's.

280. Hubert and Jan van Eyck: The Virgin Mary; The Lord; St. John the Baptist (The Ghent Altarpiece, Interior). Ghent, St. Bavo's *Copyright ACL Bruxelles.*

281. Jan van Eyck: Adam and Eve (The Ghent Altarpiece, Interior). Ghent, St. Bavo's. *Copyright ACL Bruxelles.*

282. Hubert and Jan van Eyck: Musical Angels (The Ghent Altarpiece, Interior). Ghent, St. Bavo's.

283. *a.* Jan van Eyck: The Virgin Martyrs, Detail of fig. 278; *b.* Hubert van Eyck: The Apostles, Detail of fig. 278. *Copyright ACL Bruxelles.*

284. Hubert van Eyck (?): The Annunciation. New York, Metropolitan Museum.

285. Hubert and Jan van Eyck (?): The Three Marys at the Tomb. Vierhouten, D. G. van Beuningen Collection.

286. Hubert and Jan van Eyck (?): Angel and Soldier, Details of fig. 285. *Copyright ACL Bruxelles.*

287. Follower of Jan van Eyck ("Hand H"): The Lord Enthroned in a Ceremonial Tent. *Les Très-Belles Heures de Notre Dame*, Turin Part (Destroyed), fol. 14.

288. Follower of Jan van Eyck ("Hand H"): The Agony in the Garden. *Les Très-Belles Heures de Notre Dame*, Milan Part (now Turin, Museo Civico), fol. 30 v. *Copyright ACL Bruxelles.*

289. Follower of Jan van Eyck ("Hand H"): *Pietà. Les Très-Belles Heures de Notre Dame*, Turin Part (Destroyed), fol. 49 v.

290. Follower of Jan van Eyck ("Hand H"): Calvary. *Les Très-Belles Heures de Notre Dame*, Milan Part (now Turin, Museo Civico), fol. 48 v. *Copyright ACL Bruxelles.*

291. Unknown Flemish Master: Calvary. Venice, Cà d'Oro (Museo Franchetti).

292. Nicola di Maestro Antonio (?): Calvary. Venice, Galleria dell' Accademia.

293. Follower of Jan van Eyck: The Crucifixion. Berlin, Kaiser Friedrich Museum.

294. Jan van Eyck ("Hand G"): The Virgin among Virgins. *Les Très-Belles Heures de Notre Dame*, Turin Part (Destroyed), fol. 59.

295. Jan van Eyck ("Hand G"): The Finding of the True Cross. *Les Très-Belles Heures de Notre Dame*, Milan Part (now Turin, Museo Civico), fol. 118. *Copyright ACL Bruxelles.*

296. Jan van Eyck ("Hand G"): St. Julian and His Wife Ferrying Christ over the Mouth of a River. *Les Très-Belles Heures de Notre Dame*, Turin Part (Destroyed), fol. 55 v.

297. Jan van Eyck ("Hand G"): The Prayer on the Shore. *Les Très-Belles Heures de Notre Dame*, Turin Part (Destroyed), fol. 59 v.

298. Jan van Eyck ("Hand G"): The Betrayal of Christ. *Les Très-Belles Heures de Notre Dame*, Turin Part (Destroyed), fol. 24.

299. Jan van Eyck ("Hand G"): The Birth of St. John. *Les Très-Belles Heures de Notre Dame*, Milan Part (now Turin, Museo Civico), fol. 93 v. *Copyright ACL Bruxelles.*

300. Jan van Eyck ("Hand G"): The Mass of the Dead. *Les Très-Belles Heures de Notre Dame*, Milan Part (now Turin, Museo Civico), fol. 116. *Copyright ACL Bruxelles.*

301. Jan van Eyck: Diptych. Calvary; The Last Judgment. New York, Metropolitan Museum.

302. Copy after Jan van Eyck: The Adoration of the Magi (Pen Drawing on Vellum). Berlin, Kupferstichkabinett.

303. Jan van Eyck: Details of fig. 301. *a.* Group of Mourners and the Erythrean Sibyl; *b.* Group of Damned.

304. Free Copy after Jan van Eyck: The Bearing of the Cross (Pen Drawing). Vienna, Albertina.

305. Free Copy after Jan van Eyck: The Bearing of the Cross. Budapest, Museum of Fine Arts.

306. Roger van der Weyden: Madonna Enthroned in an Aedicula. Lugano, Thyssen Collection.

307. Roger van der Weyden: Madonna Standing. Vienna, Gemäldegalerie.

308. Co-worker of Roger van der Weyden: St. Catherine. Vienna, Gemäldegalerie.

309. Roger van der Weyden and Follower: Triptych. *a.* Kneeling Donor (Follower of Roger van der Weyden), Turin, Galleria Sabauda; *b.* The Annunciation (Roger van der Weyden), Paris, Louvre; *c.* The Visitation (Follower of Roger van der Weyden), Turin, Galleria Sabauda.

310. Roger van der Weyden: The Annunciation (Central Panel of the Triptych, fig. 309). Paris, Louvre.

311. Roger van der Weyden: The Visitation. Lützschena near Leipzig, Speck von Sternburg Collection.

312. Follower of Roger van der Weyden: The Visitation (Right Wing of the Triptych, fig. 309). Turin, Galleria Sabauda.

313. Roger van der Weyden (?): St. Luke Painting the Virgin. Boston, Museum of Fine Arts. *Courtesy of the Museum of Fine Arts, Boston.*

314. Roger van der Weyden: The Descent from the Cross. Madrid, Prado (formerly Escorial).

315. Roger van der Weyden: Details of fig. 314.

316. Roger van der Weyden: The Magdalen (Fragment). London, National Gallery. *Reproduced by courtesy of the Trustees, the National Gallery, London.*

317. Roger van der Weyden: Madonna Enthroned. Madrid, Prado.

318. Roger van der Weyden: The "Miraflores Altarpiece." The Holy Family; The Lamentation; Christ Appearing to His Mother. Berlin, Kaiser Friedrich Museum.

319. Roger van der Weyden: The Holy Family, Left Panel of the "Miraflores Altarpiece." Berlin, Kaiser Friedrich Museum.

320. Roger van der Weyden: The Lamentation, Central Panel of the "Miraflores Altarpiece." Berlin, Kaiser Friedrich Museum.

321. Roger van der Weyden: Christ Appearing to His Mother, Right Panel of the "Granada Altarpiece." New York, Metropolitan Museum.

322. Roger van der Weyden: Triptych. The Magdalen; Calvary; St. Veronica. Vienna, Gemäldegalerie.

323. Roger van der Weyden: The Mater Dolorosa Embracing the Cross, Detail of fig. 322.

324. Roger van der Weyden: The Crucified Christ, Detail of Fig. 322.

325. Roger van der Weyden: The Last Judgment Altarpiece, Exterior. The Annunciation; Chancellor Nicholas Rolin; St. Sebastian; St. Anthony; Chancellor Rolin's Wife (Guigonne de Salins). Beaune, Hôtel-Dieu.

326. Roger van der Weyden: The Last Judgment Altarpiece, Interior. Beaune, Hôtel-Dieu.

327. Roger van der Weyden: Christ the Judge and St. Michael, Central Panel of the Last Judgment. Beaune, Hôtel-Dieu.

328. Roger van der Weyden: *Maria Mediatrix*, Detail of fig. 326.

329. Roger van der Weyden: Group of Damned, Detail of fig. 326.

330. Brussels, Bibliothèque Royale: Ms. 9241 (*Chroniques du Hainaut*), fol. 1. The Presentation of the Volume to Philip the Good, Probably Designed by Roger van der Weyden.

331. Roger van der Weyden: The Entombment. Florence, Uffizi.

332. Roger van der Weyden: The Madonna Standing with St. Peter, St. John the Baptist, St. Cosmas, and St. Damian. Frankfort, Städelsches Kunstinstitut.

333. Roger van der Weyden: The Triptych of Jean de Braque and Catherine of Brabant. St. John the Baptist; The Saviour between the Virgin Mary and St. John the Evangelist; The Magdalen. Paris, Louvre. *Copyright ACL Bruxelles.*

334. Roger van der Weyden: The Magdalen, Right Wing of the Triptych, fig. 333. *Copyright ACL Bruxelles.*

335. Pupil or Follower of Roger van der Weyden: The Bladelin or Middelburg Altarpiece, Exterior. The Annunciation. Berlin, Kaiser Friedrich Museum.

336. Roger van der Weyden: The Bladelin or Middelburg Altarpiece, Interior. Augustus and the Tiburtine Sibyl; The Nativity with the Donor; The Vision of the Three Magi. Berlin, Kaiser Friedrich Museum.

337. Roger van der Weyden: Central Panel of the Bladelin or Middelburg Altarpiece. The Nativity with the Donor. Berlin, Kaiser Friedrich Museum.

338. Roger van der Weyden: Wings of the Bladelin or Middelburg Altarpiece. *a.* Augustus and the Tiburtine Sibyl; *b.* The Vision of the Three Magi. Berlin, Kaiser Friedrich Museum.

339. Roger van der Weyden: Ox, Ass and Angels, Detail of fig. 337.

340. Roger van der Weyden: Augustus and the Tiburtine Sibyl, Detail of fig. 338*a.*

341. Roger van der Weyden: David Receiving the Cistern Water (fragment). Formerly Paris, Schloss Collection (Present Whereabouts Unknown).

342. Roger van der Weyden: The St. John Altarpiece. The Birth and Naming of St. John; The Baptism of Christ; The Martyrdom of St. John the Baptist. Berlin, Kaiser Friedrich Museum.

343. Roger van der Weyden: The Birth and Naming of St. John, Left Panel of the St. John Altarpiece. Berlin, Kaiser Friedrich Museum.

344. Roger van der Weyden: The Baptism of Christ, Central Panel of the St. John Altarpiece. Berlin, Kaiser Friedrich Museum.

345. Roger van der Weyden: The Martyrdom of St. John the Baptist, Right Panel of the St. John Altarpiece. Berlin, Kaiser Friedrich Museum.

346. Roger van der Weyden: Interior, Detail of fig. 343.

347. Roger van der Weyden (Executed by an Assistant): The Altarpiece of the Seven Sacraments (The "Chevrot Triptych"). Antwerp, Musée Royal des Beaux-Arts.

348. Roger van der Weyden (Executed by an Assistant): Eucharist and Calvary. Central Panel of the Altarpiece of the Seven Sacraments. Antwerp, Musée Royal des Beaux-Arts. *Copyright ACL Bruxelles.*

349. Roger van der Weyden (Executed by an Assistant): Wings of the Altarpiece of the Seven Sacraments. *a.* Baptism, Confirmation, Penance; *b.* Extreme Unction, Matrimony, Holy Orders. Antwerp, Musée Royal des Beaux-Arts. *Copyright ACL Bruxelles.*

350. Roger van der Weyden: Left Wing of a Diptych. The Virgin Mary Swooning in the Arms of St. John (Counterpart of fig. 351). Philadelphia, Pennsylvania Museum of Art (Johnson Collection). *Courtesy of the John G. Johnson Art Collection, Philadelphia.*

351. Roger van der Weyden: Right Wing of a Diptych. The Crucified Christ (Counterpart of fig. 350). Philadelphia, Pennsylvania Museum of Art, Johnson Collection. *Courtesy of the John G. Johnson Art Collection, Philadelphia.*

352. Roger van der Weyden: The "Columba Altarpiece." The Annunciation; The Adoration of the Magi; The Presentation of Christ. Munich, Alte Pinakothek.

353. Roger van der Weyden: Central Panel of the "Columba Altarpiece." The Adoration of the Magi. Munich, Alte Pinakothek.

354. Roger van der Weyden: Wings of the "Columba Altarpiece." *a.* The Annunciation; *b.* The Presentation of Christ. Munich, Alte Pinakothek.

355. Roger van der Weyden: Detail of fig. 353.

356. Roger van der Weyden: The Youngest Magus (Philip the Bold?), Detail of fig. 353.

357. Roger van der Weyden: The Crucifixion. Escorial.

358. Roger van der Weyden: The Virgin Mary, Detail of fig. 357 (Prior to Restoration). Escorial.

359. Follower of Roger van der Weyden: The Lamentation with St. Peter, St. Paul and an Episcopal Donor (Pierre de Ranchicourt?). The Hague, Mauritshuis.

360. Roger van der Weyden: Portrait of a Young Lady. Berlin, Kaiser Friedrich Museum.

361. Roger van der Weyden: Portrait of a Man at Prayer. New York, Metropolitan Museum.

362. Roger van der Weyden: Portrait of Guillaume Fillastre. Maidenhead (Berks), Stubbings House, Sir Thomas Ralph Merton Coll.

363. Roger van der Weyden: Portrait of Isabella of Portugal, Designated as the Persian Sibyl. New York, John D. Rockefeller, Jr., Collection. *Courtesy of Mr. John D. Rockefeller, Jr.*

364. Roger van der Weyden: Portrait of a Gentleman. Lugano, Thyssen Collection.

365. Roger van der Weyden: Portrait of the *Grand Bâtard de Bourgogne*. Brussels, Musée Royal. *Copyright ACL Bruxelles.*

366. Roger van der Weyden: Portrait of Francesco d'Este. New York, Metropolitan Museum.

367. Roger van der Weyden: Portrait of a Young Lady. Washington, National Gallery of Art. *Courtesy of the National Gallery of Art, Washington.*

368. Roger van der Weyden (Workshop): Madonna in Half Length (Companion Piece of fig. 369). Formerly Bruges, E. Renders Collection (Now Owned by the Belgian Government).

369. Roger van der Weyden (and Assistant): Portrait of Jean Gros (Companion Piece of fig. 368). Chicago. *Courtesy of the Art Institute, Chicago.*

370. Roger van der Weyden: Madonna in Half Length (Companion Piece of fig. 371). San Marino, Henry E. Huntington Art Gallery.

371. Roger van der Weyden: Portrait of Philippe de Croy (Companion Piece of fig. 370). Antwerp, Musée Royal des Beaux-Arts.

372. Roger van der Weyden: Madonna in Half Length (Companion Piece of fig. 373). Caen, Museum, Collection Mancel. *Photographie du Laboratoire du Musée du Louvre.*

373. Roger van der Weyden: Portrait of Laurent Froimont (Companion Piece of fig. 372). Brussels, Musée Royal. Copyright ACL Bruxelles.

374. Roger van der Weyden: Madonna in Half Length. Donaueschingen, Galerie.

375. Roger van der Weyden: Madonna in Half Length (Replica). Houston (Texas), Museum of Fine Arts, Edith A. and Percy S. Straus Collection. *Courtesy of the Museum of Fine Arts, Houston, Texas.*

376. Copy after Roger van der Weyden: Portrait of Philip the Good *en chapperon*. Bruges, Musée Communal. Copyright ACL Bruxelles.

377. Copy after Roger van der Weyden: Philip the Good in a Toupée. Antwerp, Musée Royal des Beaux-Arts. Copyright ACL Bruxelles.

378. Roger van der Weyden (Workshop): Portrait of John the Fearless (Copy after an Original of *ca.* 1415). Antwerp, Musée Royal des Beaux-Arts. Copyright ACL Bruxelles.

379. Roger van der Weyden: Portrait of Charles the Bold (Replica). Berlin, Kaiser Friedrich Museum.

380. Roger van der Weyden (Workshop): Duke John of Brabant (Silverpoint Drawing after an Earlier Original). Vierhouten, D. G. van Beuningen Collection.

381. Roger van der Weyden (Workshop): Duke Louis of Savoy (Silverpoint Drawing after a Somewhat Earlier Original). Vierhouten, D. G. van Beuningen Collection.

382. Roger van der Weyden (Workshop): Duke Philip of Brabant (Silverpoint Drawing after an Earlier Original). Formerly Amsterdam, Mannheimer Collection (Destroyed).

383. Roger van der Weyden (Workshop): Duke Philip of Nevers (Silverpoint Drawing after an Earlier Original). Formerly Amsterdam, Mannheimer Collection (Destroyed).

384. Roger van der Weyden (?): The Magdalen (Silverpoint Drawing). London, British Museum.

ILLUSTRATIONS

385. Roger van der Weyden (?): Madonna Enthroned (Pen Drawing). Rotterdam, Boymans Museum.

386. Copy after Roger van der Weyden: Madonna on a Porch (Pen Drawing). Formerly Dresden, Kupferstichkabinett.

387. Free Copy after Roger van der Weyden: The Justice of Trajan; The Justice of Herkinbald (Tapestry). Berne, Bernisches Historisches Museum.

388. Self-Portrait of Roger van der Weyden (Copy), Detail of fig. 387.

389. Arras, Bibliothèque de l'Abbaye de St.-Vaast: Ms. 266, fol. 276. Portrait of Roger van der Weyden (Pen Drawing).

390. Roger van der Weyden (Workshop): The Lamentation. Brussels, Musée Royal. *Copyright ACL Bruxelles.*

391. Copy after Roger van der Weyden: The Bearing of the Cross (Pen Drawing). Formerly Leipzig, F. Becker Collection (Present Whereabouts Unknown).

392. Copy after Roger van der Weyden: The Bearing of the Body to the Sepulchre (Pen Drawing). Paris, Louvre.

393. Copy after Roger van der Weyden (Vrancke van der Stockt?): The Descent from the Cross. Munich, Alte Pinakothek.

394. Copy after Roger van der Weyden: The Descent from the Cross with St. John the Evangelist. Nancy, Musée Municipal.

395. Follower of Quentin Massys after Roger van der Weyden: Descent from the Cross without St. John the Evangelist. Madrid, Lazaro Collection.

396. Follower of Roger van der Weyden: The Dream of Pope Sergius (Companion Piece of fig. 397). Haartekamp, Mme. von Pannwitz Collection.

397. Follower of Roger van der Weyden: The Exhumation of St. Hubert (Companion Piece of fig. 396). London, National Gallery. *Reproduced by courtesy of the Trustees, the National Gallery, London.*

398. Follower of Roger van der Weyden: Calvary. Berlin, Kaiser Friedrich Museum.

399. Follower of Roger van der Weyden: Triptych. The Donor (Oberto de Villa?); Calvary; Two Servants Carrying the Ladder. Zug, Abegg Collection.

400. Follower of Roger van der Weyden: Group of Mourners, Detail of fig. 399.

401. Follower of Roger van der Weyden: Portrait of a Young Lady, Allegedly a Demoiselle de Villa (Believed to Have Been Cut Out of the Panel, fig. 309 A). Paris, Rothschild Collection.

402. Petrus Christus: The Nativity. Washington, National Gallery of Art (Mellon Collection). *Courtesy of the National Gallery of Art, Washington.*

403. Petrus Christus: The Lamentation. Brussels, Musée Royal. *Copyright ACL Bruxelles.*

404. Petrus Christus: The Lamentation. New York, Metropolitan Museum.

405. Petrus Christus: Portrait of a Carthusian, Dated 1446. New York, Metropolitan Museum.

406. Petrus Christus: Portrait of Sir Edward Grymestone, Dated 1446. Gorhambury, St. Albans, The Earl of Verulam (on loan to the National Gallery, London). *Reproduced by permission of the Earl of Verulam.*

407. Petrus Christus: St. Eloy, Dated 1449. New York, Robert Lehman Collection.

408. Petrus Christus: Madonna Standing with St. Barbara, Venerated by Jan Vos, Prior of the Charterhouse of Genadedal ("Exeter Madonna"). Berlin, Kaiser Friedrich Museum.

409. Petrus Christus: Left Wing of a Triptych. The Annunciation; The Nativity, Dated 1452 (Counterpart of fig. 410). Berlin, Kaiser Friedrich Museum.

410. Petrus Christus: Right Wing of a Triptych. The Last Judgment, Dated 1452 (Counterpart of fig. 409). Berlin, Kaiser Friedrich Museum.

411. Petrus Christus: The Nativity. New York, Mr. Georges Wildenstein (formerly New York, Henry Goldman Collection).

ILLUSTRATIONS

412. Petrus Christus: Madonna Standing with St. Francis and St. Jerome, Dated 1457. Frankfort, Städelsches Kunstinstitut.

413. Petrus Christus: Portrait of a Young Girl. Berlin, Kaiser Friedrich Museum.

414. Dirc Bouts: The Annunciation. Madrid, Prado.

415. Dirc Bouts: The Visitation. Madrid, Prado.

416. Dirc Bouts: The Nativity. Madrid, Prado.

417. Dirc Bouts: The Adoration of the Magi. Madrid, Prado.

418. Dirc Bouts: Triptych. The Crucifixion; The Descent from the Cross; The Resurrection. Granada, Capilla Real.

419. Dirc Bouts: The Descent from the Cross, Central Panel of the Triptych, fig. 418. Granada, Capilla Real.

420. Dirc Bouts: The Entombment (Painted on Canvas). London, National Gallery. *Reproduced by courtesy of the Trustees, the National Gallery, London.*

421. Dirc Bouts: The Lamentation (Replica). Paris, Louvre.

422. Dirc Bouts: Portrait of a Young Man, Dated 1462. London, National Gallery. *Reproduced by courtesy of the Trustees, the National Gallery, London.*

423. Follower of Dirc Bouts: Self-Portrait (Silverpoint Drawing). Northampton (Mass.), Tryon Art Gallery, Smith College. *Courtesy of the Tryon Art Gallery, Northampton, Mass.*

424. Copy after Petrus Christus: Portrait of a Falconer (Silverpoint Drawing). Frankfort, Städelsches Kunstinstitut.

425. Dirc Bouts: Madonna in Half Length. New York, Metropolitan Museum.

426. Dirc Bouts: Madonna in Half Length. London, National Gallery. *Reproduced by permission of the Trustees, the National Gallery, London.*

427. Dirc Bouts: Triptych. Abraham and Melchizedek; The Gathering of Manna; The Last Supper; Elijah in the Desert; The Passover. Louvain, St. Peter's. *Copyright ACL Bruxelles.*

428. Dirc Bouts: The Last Supper, Central Panel of the Triptych, fig. 427. *Copyright ACL Bruxelles.*

429. Dirc Bouts: Elijah in the Desert, Upper Right (?) Wing of the Triptych, fig. 427. *Copyright ACL Bruxelles.*

430. Dirc Bouts: The Gathering of Manna, Lower Left (?) Wing of the Triptych, fig. 427. *Copyright ACL Bruxelles.*

431. Dirc Bouts: The Wrongful Execution of the Count (Companion Piece of fig. 432). Brussels, Musée Royal. *Copyright ACL Bruxelles.*

432. Dirc Bouts: The Ordeal of the Countess before Emperor Otto III (Companion Piece of fig. 431). Brussels, Musée Royal. *Copyright ACL Bruxelles.*

433. Follower of Dirc Bouts: Triptych Known as "The Pearl of Brabant," Central Panel. The Adoration of the Magi. Munich, Alte Pinakothek.

434. Follower of Dirc Bouts: Wings of the Triptych Known as "The Pearl of Brabant." St. John the Baptist; St. Christopher. Munich, Alte Pinakothek.

435. Albert van Ouwater: The Raising of Lazarus. Berlin, Kaiser Friedrich Museum.

436. Albert van Ouwater: Detail of fig. 435.

437. Utrecht Master of *ca.* 1460: Triptych. The Mass of St. Gregory; The Crucifixion; St. Christopher. Utrecht, Centraal Museum.

438. The Master of the Virgin Among Virgins: The Lamentation. Liverpool, Walker Art Gallery.

439. Geertgen tot Sint Jans: The Holy Kinship. Amsterdam, Rijksmuseum.

440. Geertgen tot Sint Jans: Detail of fig. 439.

441. Geertgen tot Sint Jans: Madonna in Half Length (Miniature on Vellum). Milan, Biblioteca Ambrosiana.

442. Geertgen tot Sint Jans: The Raising of Lazarus. Paris, Louvre.

443. Geertgen tot Sint Jans: St. John the Baptist in the Wilderness. Berlin, Kaiser Friedrich Museum.

444. Geertgen tot Sint Jans: The Lamentation (Originally Obverse of fig. 445). Vienna, Gemäldegalerie.

445. Geertgen tot Sint Jans: The Story of the Remains of St. John the Baptist (Originally Reverse of fig. 444). Vienna, Gemäldegalerie.

446. Geertgen tot Sint Jans: Detail of fig. 443.

447. Geertgen tot Sint Jans: Madonna in Half Length. Berlin, Kaiser Friedrich Museum.

448. Geertgen tot Sint Jans: The Nativity. London, National Gallery. *Reproduced by courtesy of the Trustees, the National Gallery, London.*

449. Geertgen tot Sint Jans: The Man of Sorrows. Utrecht, Archiepiscopal Museum.

450. Joos van Ghent: The Adoration of the Magi. New York, Metropolitan Museum.

451. Joos van Ghent: Triptych. Moses Striking the Rock; Calvary; The Brazen Serpent. Ghent, St. Bavo's. *Copyright ACL Bruxelles.*

452. Joos van Ghent: Calvary, Central Panel of the Triptych, fig. 451. *Copyright ACL Bruxelles.*

453. Joos van Ghent: Details of fig. 451. *Copyright ACL Bruxelles.*

454. Joos van Ghent: The Communion of the Apostles. Urbino, Palazzo Ducale. *Copyright ACL Bruxelles.*

455. Hugo van der Goes and Follower: Triptych. Willem van Overbeke, Commended by St. William; Madonna in Half Length (by Hugo van der Goes); Johanna de Keysere, Commended by St. John the Baptist. Frankfort, Städelsches Kunstinstitut.

456. Hugo van der Goes: Left Wing of a Diptych. The Fall of Man (Companion Piece of fig. 457). Vienna, Gemäldegalerie.

457. Hugo van der Goes: Right Wing of a Diptych. The Lamentation (Companion Piece of fig. 456; Obverse of fig. 458). Vienna, Gemäldegalerie.

458. Hugo van der Goes: St. Geneviève (Reverse of fig. 457). Vienna, Gemäldegalerie.

459. Hugo van der Goes: The "Monforte Altarpiece." The Adoration of the Magi. Berlin, Kaiser Friedrich Museum.

460. Hugo van der Goes: Detail of fig. 459.

461. Hugo van der Goes: The Portinari Altarpiece, Exterior. The Annunciation. Florence, Uffizi.

462. Hugo van der Goes: The Portinari Altarpiece, Interior. The Nativity between the Donors and Their Patron Saints. Florence, Uffizi.

463. Hugo van der Goes: Central Panel of the Portinari Altarpiece. The Nativity. Florence, Uffizi.

464. Hugo van der Goes: Wings of the Portinari Altarpiece. *a.* Tommaso, Antonio and Pigello Portinari, Commended by St. Thomas and St. Anthony; *b.* Maria and Margherita Portinari, Commended by the Magdalen and St. Margaret. Florence, Uffizi.

465. Hugo van der Goes: The Annunciate, Detail of fig. 461.

466. Hugo van der Goes: The Virgin Mary and St. Joseph on the Road to Bethlehem, Detail of fig. 464.

467. *a.* Hugo van der Goes and Follower: King James III of Scotland and the Crown Prince Commended by St. Andrew (Counterpart of fig. 467*b*, Originally Obverse of fig. 468*a*); *b.* Follower of Hugo van der Goes: Queen Margaret of Scotland Commended by St. Canute (Counterpart of fig. 467*a*, Originally Obverse of fig. 468*b*). Holyrood Palace (on loan to the National Gallery of Scotland, Edinburgh). *Reproduced with permission of the Lord Chamberlain to H. M. the Queen of Great Britain.*

468. *a.* Hugo van der Goes: The Trinity of the Broken Body (Companion Piece

of fig. 468*b*, Originally Reverse of fig. 467*a*); *b*. Hugo van der Goes: Sir Edward Bonkil and an Angelic Organist (Counterpart of fig. 468*a*, Originally Reverse of fig. 467*b*). Holyrood Palace (on loan to the National Gallery of Scotland, Edinburgh). *Reproduced with permission of the Lord Chamberlain to H. M. the Queen of Great Britain.*

469. Hugo van der Goes: St. Andrew, Detail of fig. 467*a*. *Reproduced with permission of the Lord Chamberlain to H. M. the Queen of Great Britain.*

470. Hugo van der Goes: A Donor Commended by St. John the Baptist (Fragment). Baltimore, Walters Art Gallery. *Courtesy of the Walters Art Gallery, Baltimore.*

471. Hugo van der Goes: The Nativity. Berlin, Kaiser Friedrich Museum.

472. Hugo van der Goes: Adoring Shepherds, Detail of fig. 471.

473. Hugo van der Goes: The Death of the Virgin. Bruges, Musée Communal. *Copyright ACL Bruxelles.*

474. Follower of Hugo van der Goes: The Adoration of the Magi, Central Panel of the "Liechtenstein Altarpiece." Vienna, Liechtenstein Gallery.

475. Follower of Hugo van der Goes: The Nativity. Wilton House, The Earl of Pembroke.

476. Hans Memlinc: Triptych. St. John the Baptist; The Madonna Enthroned with the Donors (Sir John Donne of Kidwelly and His Wife), St. Catherine, and St. Barbara; St. John the Evangelist. Chatsworth, Duke of Devonshire Collection (now Chatsworth Estates Company).

477. Hans Memlinc: Portrait of a Young Fiancée (Companion Piece of fig. 478). New York, Metropolitan Museum.

478. Hans Memlinc: Two Horses Standing in a Brook (Companion Piece of fig. 477). Vierhouten, D. G. van Beuningen Collection.

479. Hans Memlinc: The Adoration of the Magi. Madrid, Prado.

480. Hans Memlinc: Portrait of a Young Italian. Antwerp, Musée Royal des Beaux-Arts.

481. Hans Memlinc: The Madonna Enthroned between Two Musical Angels. Washington, National Gallery of Art (Mellon Collection). *Courtesy of the National Gallery of Art, Washington.*

482. Gerard David: The Lord Blessing (Top Piece of a Triptych or Polyptch). Paris, Louvre.

483. Gerard David: Interior of a Triptych. Jan de Sedano and His Son, Commended by St. John the Baptist; The Madonna Enthroned between Two Musical Angels; Jeanne de Sedano, Commended by St. John the Evangelist. Paris, Louvre.

484. Gerard David: The Virgin among Virgins. Rouen, Musée de la Ville.

485. Gerard David: The Bethrothal of St. Catherine. London, National Gallery. *Reproduced by courtesy of the Trustees, the National Gallery, London.*

486. Gerard David: St. Catherine, Detail of fig. 485. *Reproduced by courtesy of the Trustees, the National Gallery, London.*

487. Jan Gossart: The Madonna in a Church. Rome, Galleria Doria.

488. Jan Gossart: Deësis. Madrid, Prado.

489. Quentin Massys: Madonna Enthroned. Brussels, Musée Royal. *Copyright ACL Bruxelles.*

490. Quentin Massys: Madonna Standing. London, Count A. Seilern Collection. *Courtesy of Count Seilern.*

491. Quentin Massys: The Money Changer and His Wife. Paris, Louvre.

492. Quentin Massys: Portrait of an Elderly Man, Dated 1513. Paris, Musée Jacquemart-André.

493. Quentin Massys: "The Ugly Duchess." London, National Gallery. *Reproduced by courtesy of the Trustees, the National Gallery, London.*

ILLUSTRATIONS

PLATES

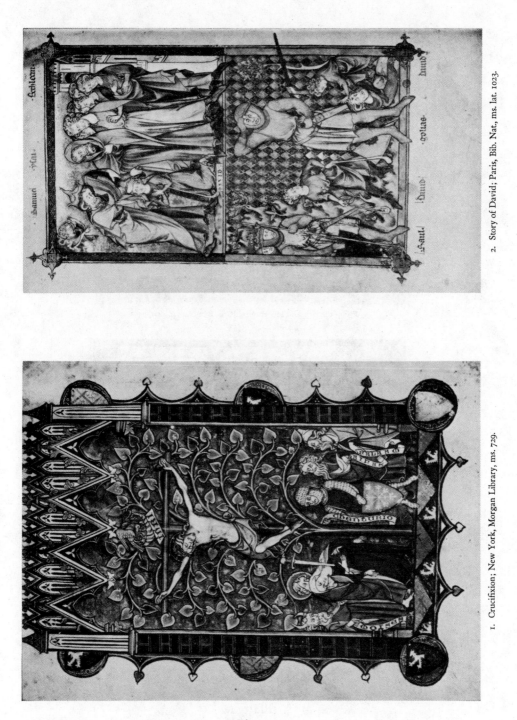

2. Story of David; Paris, Bib. Nat, ms. lat. 1023.

1. Crucifixion; New York, Morgan Library, ms. 729.

Plate 1.

3. Philip the Fair and His Family; Paris, Bib. Nat., ms. lat. 8504.

4. Job, His Wife and a Friend; Paris, Bib. de l'Arsenal, ms. 5059.

Plate 2.

5. Annunciation; Paris, Rothschild Coll., Hours of Jeanne d'Evreux. 6. Duccio, Annunciation of the Virgin's Death; Siena, Opera del Duomo.
7. Lamentation; Paris, Rothschild Coll., Hours of Jeanne d'Evreux. 8. Duccio, Lamentation; Siena, Opera del Duomo.

Plate 3.

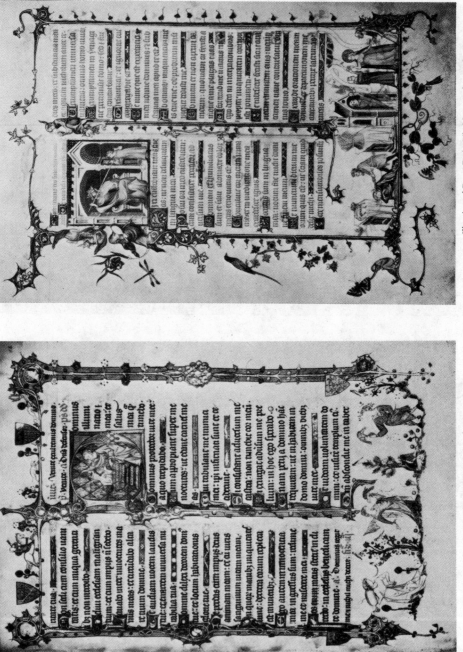

10. Illuminated Page; Paris, Bib. Nat., ms. lat. 1048.

9. Illuminated Page; Verdun, Bib. Municipale, ms. 107.

Plate 4.

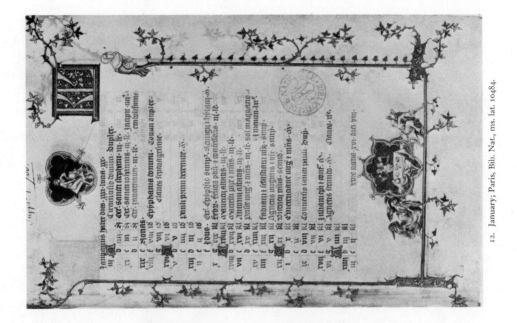

12. January; Paris, Bib. Nat., ms. lat. 10484.

11. December; Paris, Bib. Nat., ms. lat. 10483.

Plate 5.

13. February; Paris, Rothschild Coll.

14. March; Paris, Rothschild Coll.

15. February; Hours of Bonne of Luxembourg
(Location Unknown).

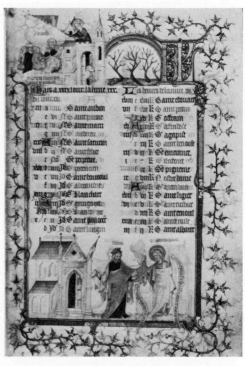

16. March; Paris, Bib. Nat., ms. lat. 18014.

Plate 6.

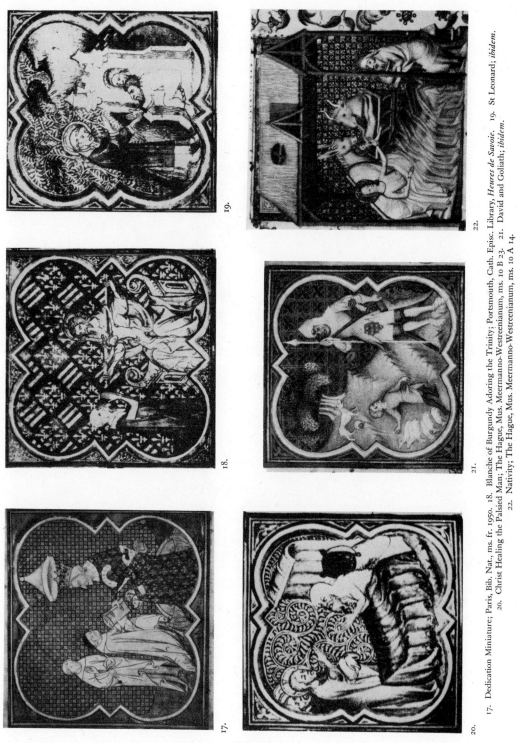

17. Dedication Miniature; Paris, Bib. Nat., ms. fr. 1950. 18. Blanche of Burgundy Adoring the Trinity; Portsmouth, Cath. Episc. Library, *Heures de Savoie*. 19. St Leonard; *ibidem*. 20. Christ Healing the Palsied Man; The Hague, Mus. Meermanno-Westreenianum, ms. 10 B 23. 21. David and Goliath; The Hague, Mus. Meermanno-Westreenianum, ms. 10 A 14. 22. Nativity; The Hague, Mus. Meermanno-Westreenianum, ms. 10 A 14.

Plate 7.

23. Dedicatory Inscription and Miniature; The Hague, Mus. Meermanno-Westreenianum, ms. 10 B 23.

Plate 8.

24. Lot and His Daughters; Paris, Bib. Nat., ms. fr. 15397.

25. Revelation XIV, 13 (Tapestry); Angers, Musée des Tapisseries.

Plate 9.

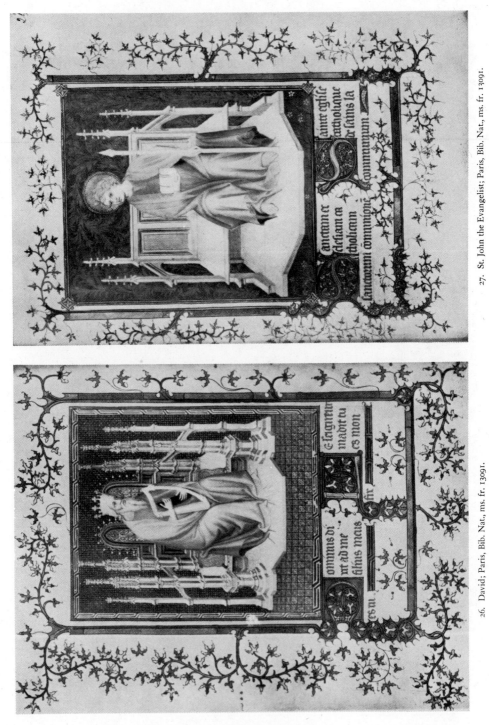

27. St. John the Evangelist; Paris, Bib. Nat., ms. fr. 13091.

26. David; Paris, Bib. Nat., ms. fr. 13091.

Plate 10.

28. Jean le Bon; Paris, Louvre.

Plate 11.

29. *Parement de Narbonne, Central Section; Paris, Louvre.*

Plate 12.

31. Baptism of Christ (Enlarged); Paris, Bib. Nat, ms. lat. 18014.

30. Matins Page (Reduced); Paris, Bib. Nat, ms. lat. 18014.

Plate 13.

32. Annunciation; Paris, Bib. Nat., ms. lat. 1804.   33. St. John in the Wilderness; *ibidem.*   34. Lamentation; *ibidem.*   35. Lamentation; *ibidem.*   36. Derision of Christ; *ibidem.*

Plate 14.

38. Pisan Master, Nativity; Pisa, Museo Civico.

37. Nativity; Turin, Museo Civico, *Très-Belles Heures*.

Plate 15.

39. Descent from the Cross and Lamentation; Paris, Rothschild Collection, *Très-Belles Heures*.

Plate 16.

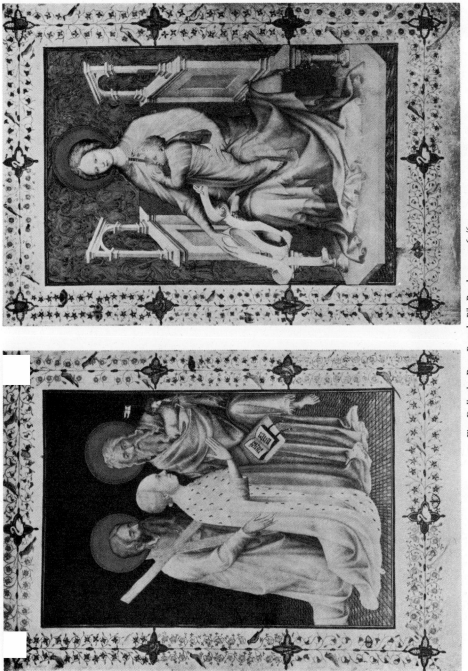

40. First Dedication Page; Brussels, Bib. Royale, ms. 11060/61.

Plate 17.

42. Annunciation; Brussels, Bib. Royale, ms. 11060/61.

41. Second Dedication Page; Brussels, Bib. Royale, ms. 11060/61.

Plate 18.

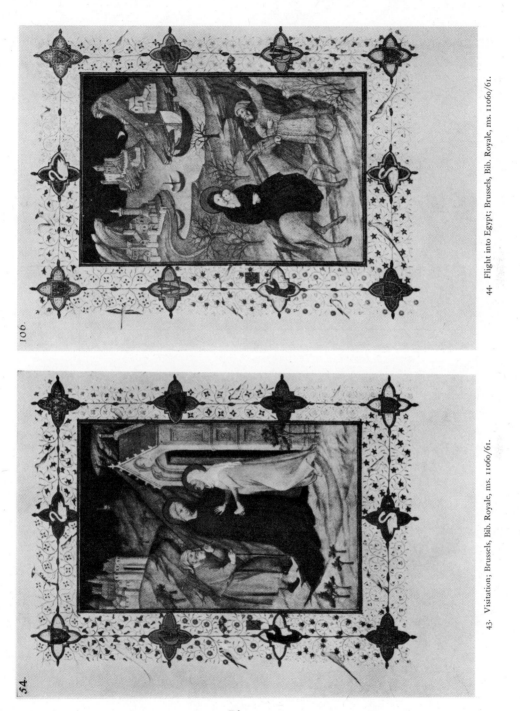

44. Flight into Egypt; Brussels, Bib. Royale, ms. 11060/61.

43. Visitation; Brussels, Bib. Royale, ms. 11060/61.

Plate 19.

46. Simone Martini, Bearing of the Cross; Paris, Louvre.

45. Bearing of the Cross; Brussels, Bib. Royale, ms. 11060/61.

186.

Plate 20.

47. Illuminated Page; Paris, Bib. Nat., ms. lat. 919.

Plate 21.

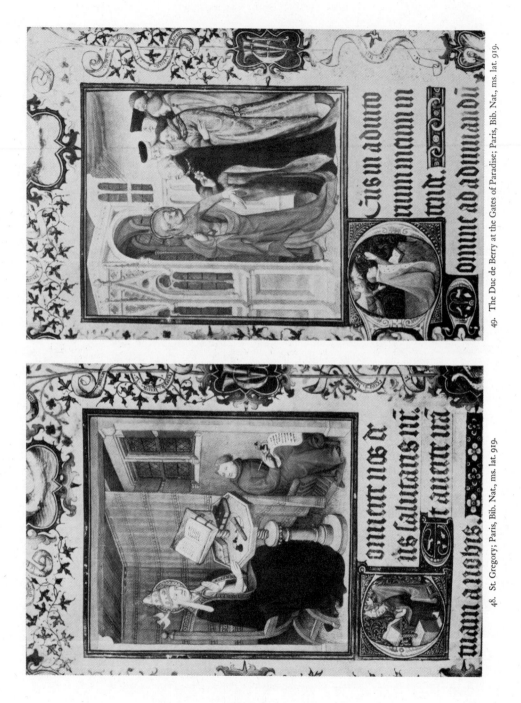

49. The Duc de Berry at the Gates of Paradise; Paris, Bib. Nat, ms. lat. 919.

48. St. Gregory; Paris, Bib. Nat, ms. lat 919.

Plate 22.

Cy apres deuile du chien dovsel et de toute sa nature.

50.   The Bird Hound; Paris, Bib. de l'Arsenal, ms. 616.

a tenir et la contree ou les tartars demourent

51.   The Land of the Tartars; Paris, Bib. Nat., ms. fr. 12201.

Plate 23.

52. Crucifixion; Brussels, Bib. Royale, ms. 9125.

Plate 24.

53. Penthesilea; Paris, Bib. Nat., ms. fr. 598.

56. *Caritas Romana*; Paris, Bib. Nat., ms. fr. 598.

55. Sappho; Paris, Bib. Nat., ms. fr. 598.

54. Antiope and Oreithyia; Paris, Bib. Nat., ms. fr. 12420.

Plate 25.

57. Creation of Adam; Paris, Bib. de l'Arsenal, ms. 5057.

58. Judgment and Parables of Solomon; Paris, Bib. de l'Arsenal, ms. 5058.

Plate 26.

59. Visitation; Paris, Mus. Jacquemart-André, Boucicaut Hours.

Plate 27.

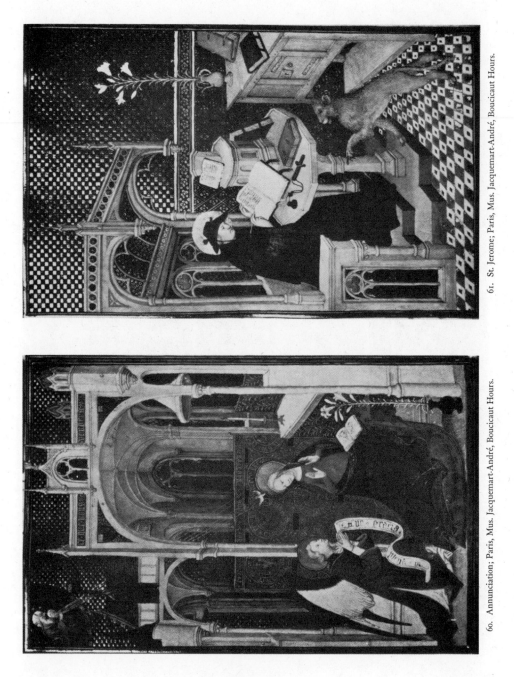

61. St. Jerome; Paris, Mus. Jacquemart-André, Boucicaut Hours.

60. Annunciation; Paris, Mus. Jacquemart-André, Boucicaut Hours.

Plate 28.

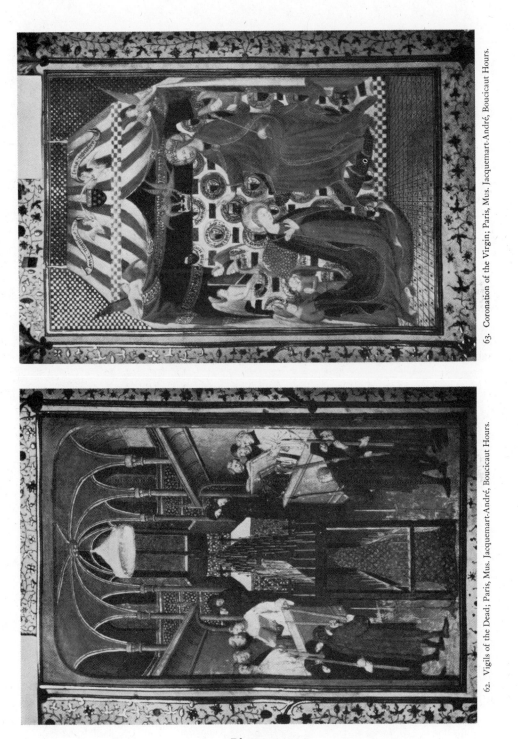

63. Coronation of the Virgin; Paris, Mus. Jacquemart-André, Boucicaut Hours.

62. Vigils of the Dead; Paris, Mus. Jacquemart-André, Boucicaut Hours.

Plate 29.

65. Boucicaut Venerating St. Catherine; Paris, Mus. Jacquemart-André, Boucicaut Hours.

64. Dedication Page; Paris, Mus. Jacquemart-André, Boucicaut Hours.

Plate 30.

Plate 31.

69. Charles VI and Pierre Salmon; Geneva, Bib. Publique et Universitaire, ms. fr. 165.

68. Scene from *Dialogues* of Pierre Salmon; Paris, Bib. Nat., ms. fr. 23279.

Plate 32.

70. Vigils of the Dead; Paris, Bib. Nat.,
ms. lat. 10538.

71. Birth of St. John; Bourges, Bib. de la Ville,
ms. 34.

72. Nativity; Paris, Bib. Nat.,
ms. lat. 10538.

73. Nativity; Baltimore, Walters Art Gallery,
ms. 260.

Plate 33.

74. Annunciation; Paris, Bib. Nat., ms. lat. 1161.

75. *Piété Nostre Seigneur*; Paris, Bib. Nat., ms. lat. 1161.

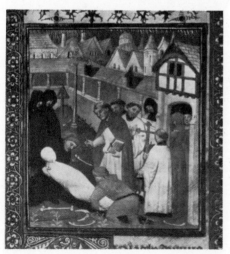

76. Funeral Service; Paris, Bib. Nat., ms. lat. 1161.

77. Journey of the Magi; Paris, Bib. Nat., ms. fr. 2810.

Plate 34.

78. Donatrix Venerating the Madonna; Paris, Bib. Nat., ms. lat. 1161.

79. Coronation of Hannibal; Paris, Bib. Nat., ms. fr. 259.

Plate 35.

80. Annunciation; Chantilly, Mus. Condé, *Très Riches Heures*.

Plate 36.

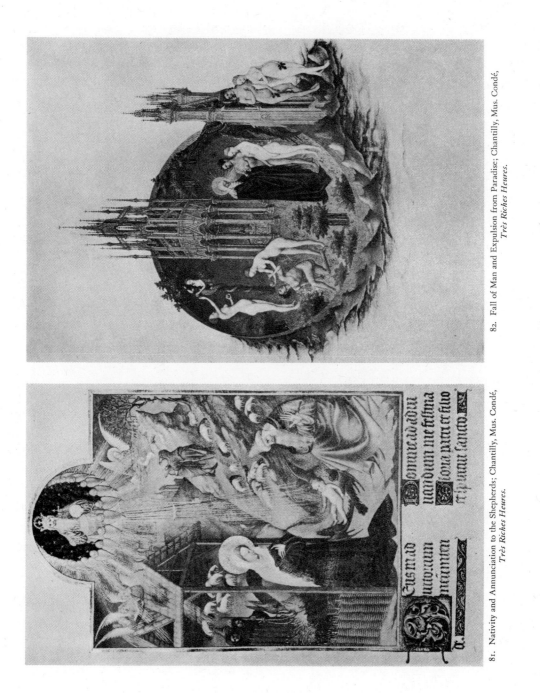

82. Fall of Man and Expulsion from Paradise; Chantilly, Mus. Condé, *Très Riches Heures.*

81. Nativity and Annunciation to the Shepherds; Chantilly, Mus. Condé, *Très Riches Heures.*

Plate 37.

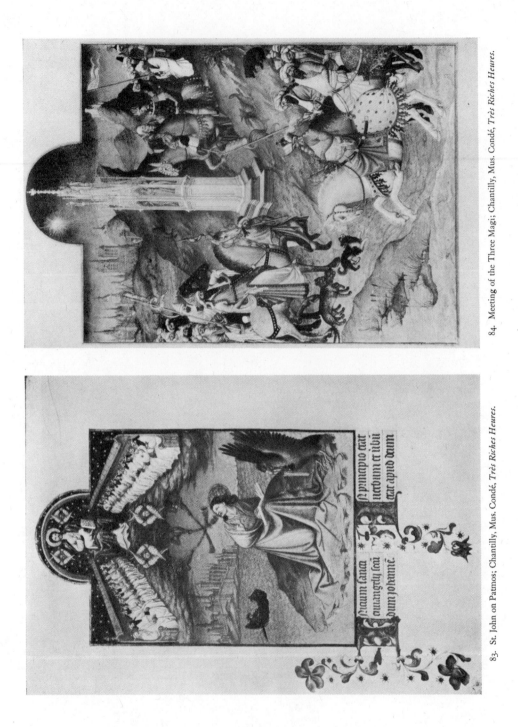

84. Meeting of the Three Magi; Chantilly, Mus. Condé, *Très Riches Heures.*

83. St. John on Patmos; Chantilly, Mus. Condé, *Très Riches Heures.*

Plate 38.

85. Constantine (Medal);
Vienna, Kunsthistorisches Museum.

86. Giotto, Stigmatization of St. Francis; Florence, Santa Croce.

Plate 39.

87. Christ at Gethsemane; Chantilly, Mus. Condé, *Très Riches Heures.*

Plate 40.

89. February; Chantilly, Mus. Condé, *Très Riches Heures.*

88. January; Chantilly, Mus. Condé, *Très Riches Heures.*

Plate 41.

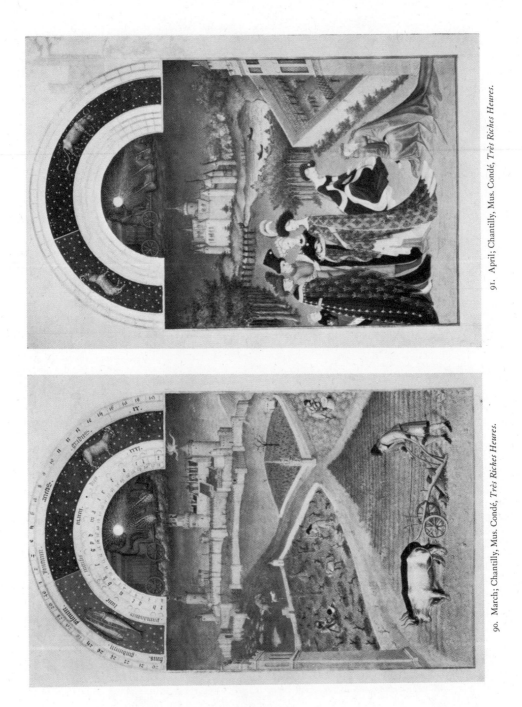

91. April; Chantilly, Mus. Condé, *Très Riches Heures.*

90. March; Chantilly, Mus. Condé, *Très Riches Heures.*

Plate 42.

92. Franco-Flemish Master of *ca.* 1420, Young Lady; Washington, National Gallery.

93. Group of Ladies; Chantilly, Mus. Condé, *Très Riches Heures.*

94. April Master of the *Très Riches Heures*, John the Fearless (Copy); Paris, Louvre.

95. Detail of fig. 91. Chantilly, Mus. Condé, *Très Riches Heures.*

Plate 43.

96. Madonna; Cambridge, Mass., Harvard University Library, De Buz Hours.

Plate 44.

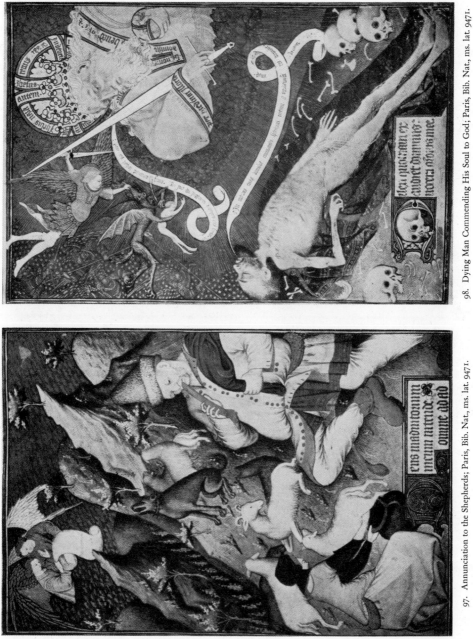

Plate 45.

99. Valencian Master of *ca.* 1420, the "Carrand Diptych"; Florence, Museo Nazionale.

Plate 46.

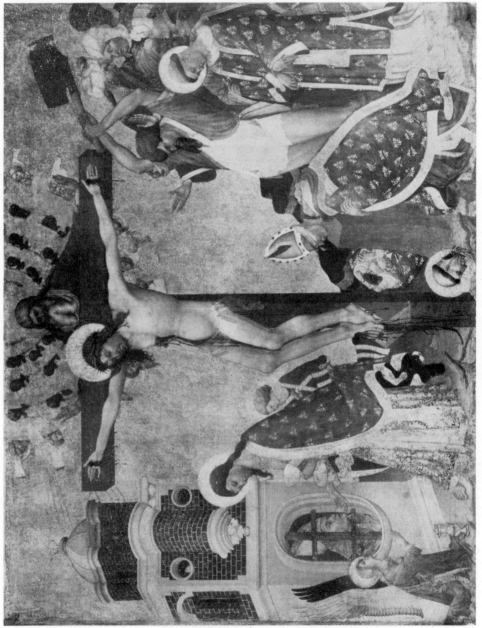

100. Jean Malouel and Henri Bellechose, Martyrdom of St. Denis; Paris, Louvre.

Plate 47.

101. Jean Malouel, Trinity with the Virgin and St. John the Evangelist;
Paris, Louvre.

102. French Master of *ca.* 1410, Coronation of the Virgin; Berlin,
Kaiser Friedrich Museum.

Plate 48.

103. Utrecht Master of 1363, Calvary of Hendrik van Rijn; Antwerp, Musée Royal.

Plate 49.

104. Melchior Broederlam, Annunciation and Visitation; Dijon, Musée de la Ville.

Plate 50.

105. Melchior Broederlam, Presentation of Christ and Flight into Egypt; Dijon, Musée de la Ville.

Plate 51.

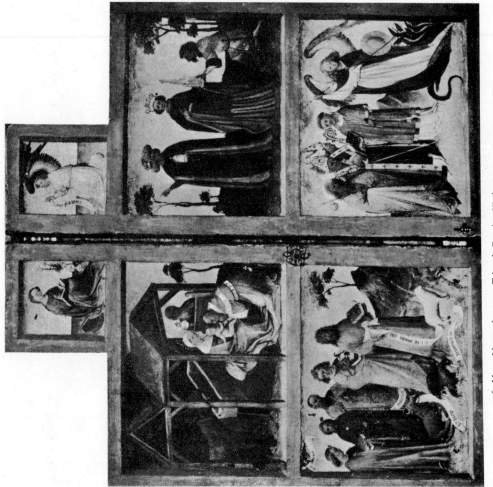

106. Mosan Master of *ca. 1415*, Triptych, Exterior; Vierhouten, van Beuningen Coll.

Plate 52.

107. Mosan Master of *ca.* 1415, Triptych, Interior; Vierhouten, van Beuningen Coll.

Plate 53.

108 a.

108 b.   108 c.

108. Guelders(?) Master of 1400–1410, Quadriptych, Left Half; *a.* and *b.* Baltimore,
Walters Art Gallery; *c.* Antwerp, Musée Mayer van den Bergh.

Plate 54.

109 a.

109 b.   109 c.

109. Guelders (?) Master of 1400–1410, Quadriptych, Right Half; *a.* and *c.* Antwerp,
Musée Mayer van den Bergh; *b.* Baltimore, Walters Art Gallery.

Plate 55.

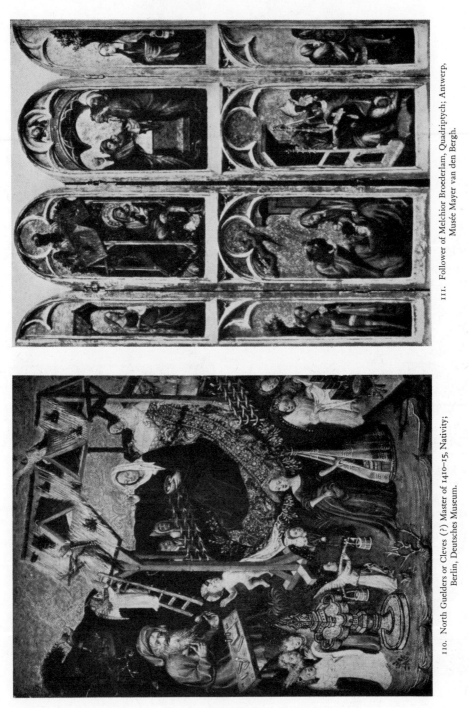

III. Follower of Melchior Broederlam, Quadriptych; Antwerp, Musée Mayer van den Bergh.

110. North Guelders or Cleves (?) Master of 1410–15, Nativity; Berlin, Deutsches Museum.

Plate 56.

112. Brabantine Master of *ca.* 1400, Birth of the Virgin; Brussels, Musée Royal.

113. Bruges Master of *ca.* 1400, Calvary of the Tanners: Bruges, St.-Sauveur.

Plate 57.

114. Alexander the Great on His Deathbed; Brussels,
Bib. Royale, ms. 205 A.

116. Emperor, Knight and Husbandman;
New York, Morgan Library, ms. 691.

118. Last Judgment; Baltimore, Walters
Art Gallery, ms. 185.

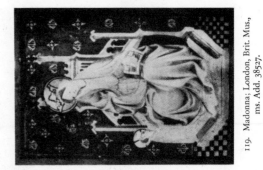

115. Creation of the World; Baltimore, Walters Art Gallery,
ms. 171.

117. Christ in the Winepress; London, Brit. Mus.,
ms. Add. 22288.

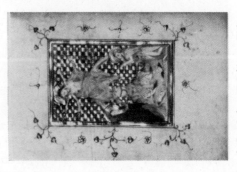

119. Madonna; London, Brit. Mus.,
ms. Add. 38527.

Plate 58.

120. Mary, Duchess of Guelders, and Betrayal of Christ; Berlin, Staatsbibliothek, Cod. germ. 4° 42.

Plate 59.

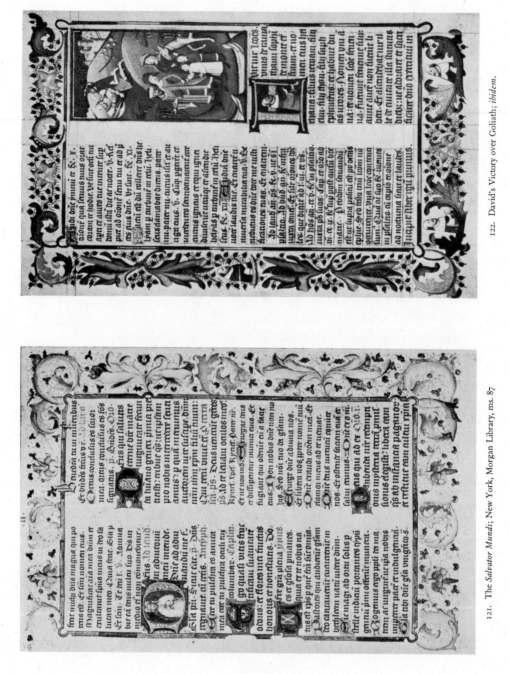

Plate 60.

121. The *Salvator Mundi*; New York, Morgan Library, ms. 87

122. David's Victory over Goliath; *ibidem*.

123. The Brazen Serpent; New York,
Morgan Library, ms. 87.

124. St. John the Baptist Preaching;
ibidem.

125. The Prophet Jonah;
ibidem.

126. Coronation of the
Virgin; *ibidem.*

Plate 61.

127. Nativity; Formerly Kottbus, Bum Collection, Book of Hours.

128. Adoration of the Magi; The Hague, Mus. Meermanno-Westreenianum, ms. 10 E 1.

129. Crucifixion; Nordkirchen, Duke of Arenberg, Book of Hours.

130. Descent from the Cross; Nordkirchen, Duke of Arenberg, Book of Hours.

Plate 62.

131. Annunciation; Liége, Bib. Universitaire, ms. 35.

132. Nativity; *ibidem*.

133. Chorus of Angels; London, Brit. Mus.,
ms. Egerton 859.

134. Susanna and the Elders;
ibidem.

Plate 63.

135. Saturn in His Mansions; New York, Morgan Library, ms. 785.

Plate 64.

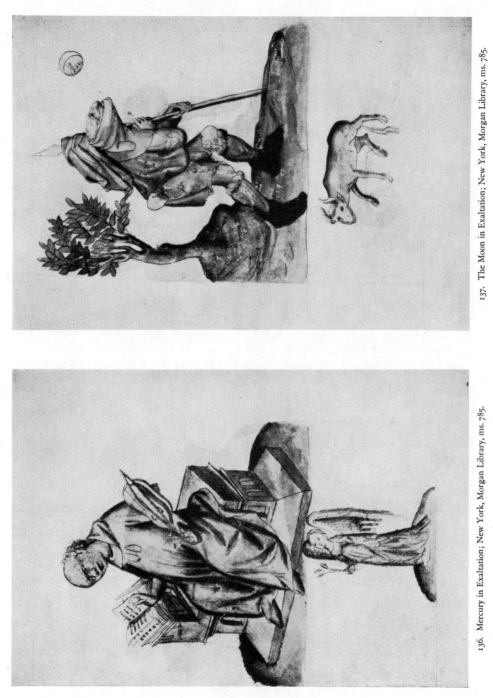

137. The Moon in Exaltation; New York, Morgan Library, ms. 785.

136. Mercury in Exaltation; New York, Morgan Library, ms. 785.

Plate 65.

141. The Sermon on the Mount; Brussels, Bib. Royale, ms. 11041.

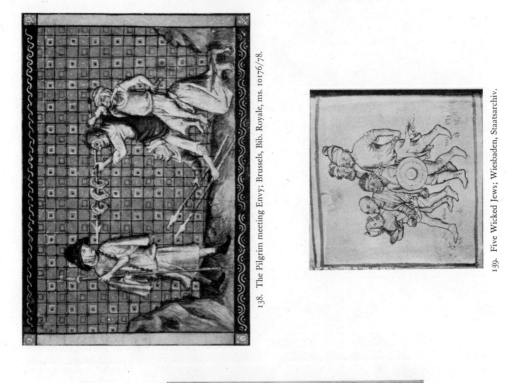

138. The Pilgrim meeting Envy; Brussels, Bib. Royale, ms. 1076/78.

139. Five Wicked Jews; Wiesbaden, Staatsarchiv.

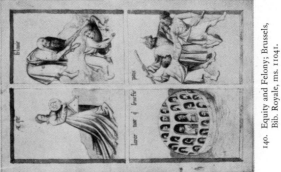

140. Equity and Felony; Brussels, Bib. Royale, ms. 11041.

Plate 66.

147. Last Supper; Brussels, Bib. Royale, ms. II, 7831.

148. Christ Appearing to His Mother; *ibidem.*

149. Dedication Page; Tournai, Bib. Municipale, ms. 42.

145. Annunciation; Paris, Bib. Nat., ms. lat. 1364.

146. Baptism of Christ; Paris, Bib. Nat., ms. lat. 1364.

142. Annunciation; Brussels, Bib. Royale, ms. II, 7831.

143. Nativity; *ibidem.*

144. Entry into Jerusalem; *ibidem.*

Plate 67.

150. Revelation I; Paris, Bib. Nat., ms. néerl. 3.

Plate 68.

152. Revelation VIII; Paris, Bib. Nat., ms. néerl. 3.

151. Revelation II, III; Paris, Bib. Nat., ms. néerl. 3.

Plate 69.

Plate 70.

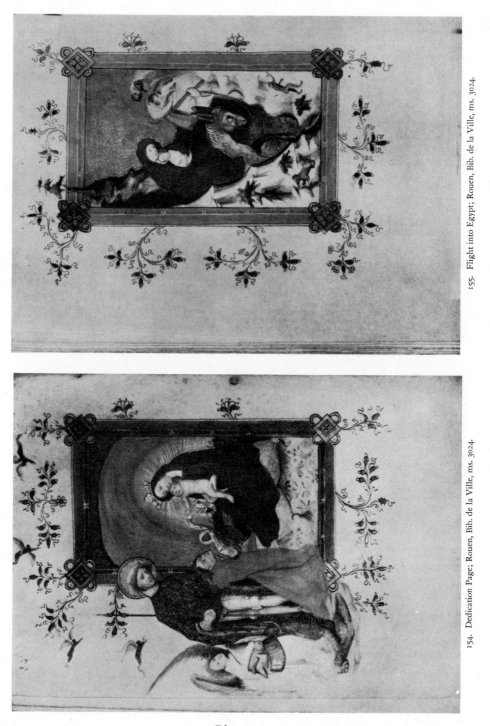

155. Flight into Egypt; Rouen, Bib. de la Ville, ms. 3024.

154. Dedication Page; Rouen, Bib. de la Ville, ms. 3024.

Plate 71.

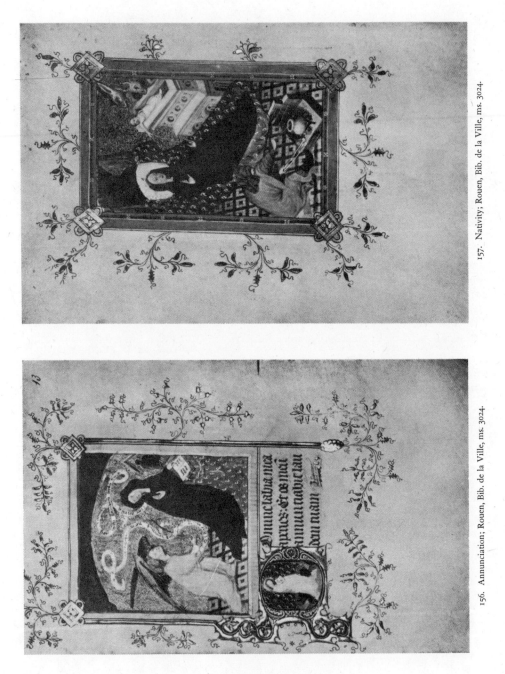

157. Nativity; Rouen, Bib. de la Ville, ms. 3024.

156. Annunciation; Rouen, Bib. de la Ville, ms. 3024.

Plate 72.

159. The Madonna, St. Catherine and St. Agnes in the Garden of Paradise; Carpentras, Bib. de la Ville, ms. 57.

158. The Holy Face and the Garden of Paradise; Rouen, Bib. de la Ville, ms. 3024.

Plate 73.

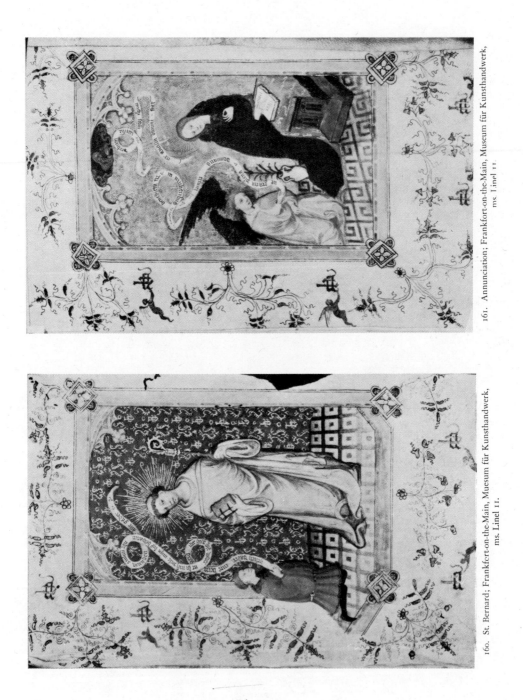

161. Annunciation; Frankfort-on-the-Main, Museum für Kunsthandwerk, ms. Linel 11.

160. St. Bernard; Frankfort-on-the-Main, Museum für Kunsthandwerk, ms. Linel 11.

Plate 74.

165. Annunciation; Indianapolis, Dr. Clowes Coll., Book of Hours.

162. St. Christopher; Oxford, Bodleian Library, ms. Can. Lit. 118.

164. Melchior Broederlam; Detail of fig. 104.

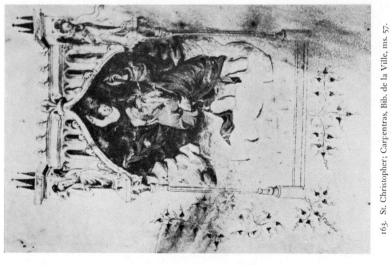

163. St. Christopher; Carpentras, Bib. de la Ville, ms. 57.

Plate 75.

169

166. Immaculate Conception; London, Brit. Mus., ms. Add. 29704.
167. St. Louis; *ibidem*.
168. St. John the Evangelist; London, Brit. Mus., ms. Add. 16998.
169. Story of St. Martin; London, Brit. Mus., ms. Add. 29704.
170. Annunciation; London, Brit. Mus., ms. Add. 16998.
171. Portrait of the Owner; *ibidem*.
172. Madonna of Humility; *ibidem*.

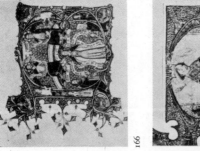

166

167

168

Plate 76.

174. Annunciation; London, Brit. Mus., ms. Royal 2 A XVIII.

173. St. Christopher; London, Brit. Mus., ms. Royal 2 A XVIII.

Plate 77.

175. Annunciation; London, Lambeth Palace Library, ms. 69.
177. Anointing of David; *ibidem.*   178. Entombment; *ibidem.*
180. Nativity; *ibidem.*

176. Annunciation; London, Brit. Mus., ms. Add. 42131.
179. Annunciation; London; Brit. Mus., ms. Add. 18213.

Plate 78.

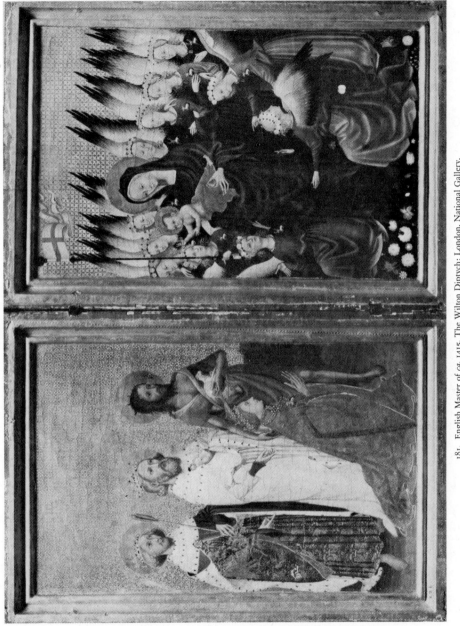

Plate 79.

182. Nativity; Paris, Bib. Nat., ms. lat. Nouv. Acq. 3055.

183. St. Christopher; *ibidem*.

184. Derision of Christ; *ibidem*.

185. St. Andrew; *ibidem*.

Plate 80.

187. St. Christopher and St. Anthony;
Baltimore, Walters Art Gallery, ms. 166.

186. Daniel in the Lions' Den Venerated by Daniel Rym;
Baltimore, Walters Art Gallery, ms. 166.

Plate 81.

188. Bearing of the Cross; Baltimore,
Walters Art Gallery, ms. 166.

189. Betrayal of Christ; Baltimore, Walters
Art Gallery, ms. 166.

190. St. Barbara; Baltimore, Walters
Art Gallery, ms. 170.

191. Rest on the Flight into Egypt; Baltimore,
Walters Art Gallery, ms. 211.

Plate 82.

192. St. John the Baptist; New York, Morgan Library,
ms. 439.

193. St. George; Providence, R. I., J. C. Brown
Library, ms. 3.

194. St. George; Lisbon, National Archives,
Duarte Hours.

195. St. George; Bruges, Grand Séminaire,
ms. vol. 72/175.

Plate 83.

Plate 84.

198. Master of Flémalle (?), Madonna of Humility; Berlin, Kaiser Friedrich Museum.

197. Master of Flémalle; Entombment of Christ; Detail of fig. 196.

Plate 85.

199. Master of Flémalle, Betrothal of the Virgin; Madrid, Prado.

Plate 86.

200. Master of Flémalle, St. James the Great and St. Clare; Madrid, Prado.

Plate 87.

201. Master of Flémalle, Nativity; Dijon, Musée de la Ville.

Plate 88.

202. Master of Flémalle; Detail of fig. 201.

Plate 89.

203. Master of Flémalle, Madonna; London, National Gallery.

Plate 90.

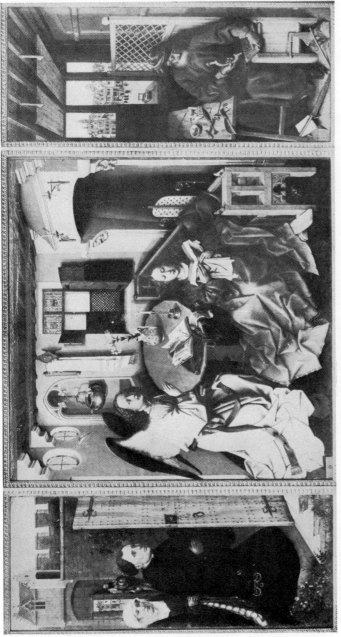

204. Master of Flémalle, The "Mérode Altarpiece"; Formerly Westerloo-Tongerloo, Princess de Mérode.

Plate 91.

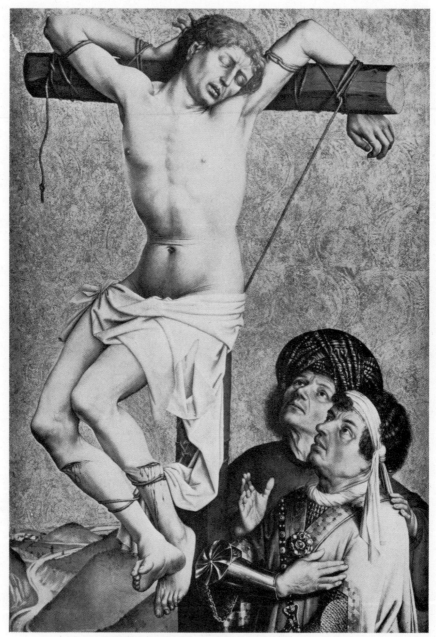

205. Master of Flémalle, The Bad Thief; Frankfort-on-the-Main, Städelsches Kunstinstitut.

Plate 92.

208. Master of Flémalle, St. Veronica; Frankfort-on-the-Main, Städelsches Kunstinstitut.

207. Master of Flémalle, Trinity; Frankfort-on-the-Main, Städelsches Kunstinstitut.

206. Master of Flémalle, Madonna; Frankfort-on-the-Main, Städelsches Kunstinstitut.

Plate 93.

209. Master of Flémalle, Madonna in a Glory; Aix-en-Provence,
Mus. Granet.

Plate 94.

210. Master of Flémalle, Trinity; Leningrad, Hermitage.

Plate 95.

211. Master of Flémalle, Madonna at the Fireplace; Leningrad, Hermitage.

Plate 96.

212. Master of Flémalle, The Werl Altarpiece,
Left Wing; Madrid, Prado.

213. Master of Flémalle, The Werl Altarpiece,
Right Wing; Madrid, Prado.

Plate 97.

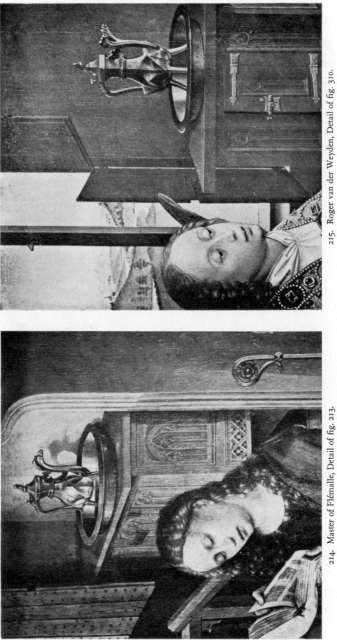

215. Roger van der Weyden, Detail of fig. 310.

214. Master of Flémalle, Detail of fig. 213.

Plate 98.

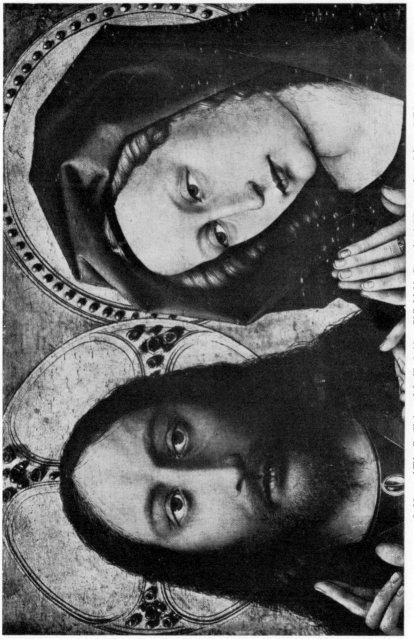

216. Master of Flémalle, Christ and the Virgin Mary; Philadelphia, Pennsylvania Museum of Art, Johnson Coll.

Plate 99.

217. Master of Flémalle, Portrait of a Gentleman; London, National Gallery.

Plate 100.

218. Master of Flémalle, Portrait of a Lady; London, National Gallery.

Plate 101.

219. Master of Flémalle (?), Portrait of a Musician; New York, Mrs. J. Magnin Coll.

Plate 102.

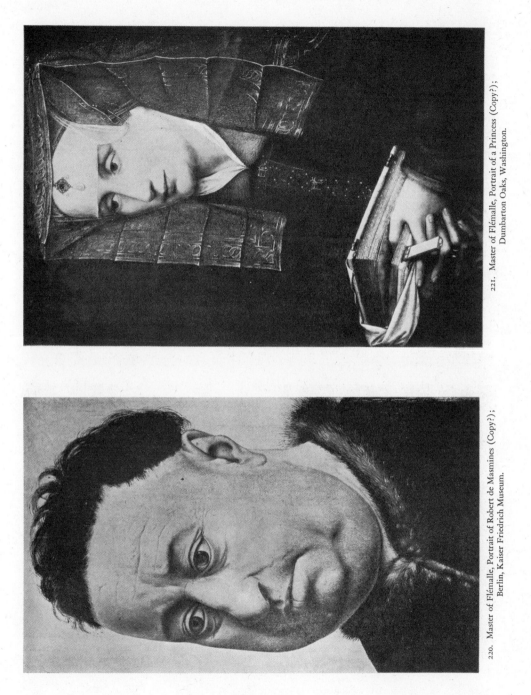

221. Master of Flémalle, Portrait of a Princess (Copy?);
Dumbarton Oaks, Washington.

220. Master of Flémalle, Portrait of Robert de Masmines (Copy?);
Berlin, Kaiser Friedrich Museum.

Plate 103.

222. Master of Flémalle, Madonna in an Apse
(Copy); New York, Metropolitan Museum.

223. Master of Flémalle, Adoration of the Magi
(Copy); Berlin, Kaiser Friedrich Museum.

224. Master of Flémalle, Vengeance of Tomyris (Copy); Berlin,
Kaiser Friedrich Museum.

225. Master of Flémalle, Jael Slaying Sisera (Pen,
Copy); Braunschweig, Landesmuseum.

Plate 104.

226. Master of Flémalle Madonna of Humility
(Copy); Brussels, G. Müller Coll.

227. Master of Flémalle, Mass of St. Gregory (Copy);
New York, E. Schwarz Coll.

228. Colin de Coter (Probably after the Master of
Flémalle), St. Luke Painting the Virgin;
Vieure, Church.

229. Gerard David (after the Master of
Flémalle), Crucifixion; Lugano,
Thyssen Coll.

Plate 105.

230. Master of Flémalle Triptych (Copy); Liverpool, Walker Art Gallery.

Plate 106.

Plate 107.

232. Jacques Daret, Visitation; Berlin, Kaiser Friedrich
Museum.

233. Jacques Daret, Nativity; Lugano,
Thyssen Coll.

234. Jacques Daret, Adoration of the Magi; Berlin,
Kaiser Friedrich Museum.

235. Jacques Daret, Presentation of Christ; Paris,
Petit Palais.

Plate 108.

236. Jan van Eyck, Madonna in a Church; Berlin,
Kaiser Friedrich Museum.

Plate 109.

237. Jan van Eyck; Detail of fig. 236.

Plate 110.

238. Jan van Eyck, Annunciation; Washington,
National Gallery.

Plate 111.

239. Jan van Eyck; Detail of fig. 238.

Plate 112.

240. Jan van Eyck, Triptych; Dresden, Gemäldegalerie.

Plate 113.

241. Jan van Eyck, Madonna; Central Panel of fig. 240.

Plate 114.

242. Jan van Eyck Annunciation; Exterior Wings of fig. 240.

Plate 115.

243. Jan van Eyck, Madonna; Melbourne, National Gallery.

Plate 116.

244. Jan van Eyck, Madonna of Chancellor Rolin; Paris, Louvre.

Plate 117.

245. Jan van Eyck; Detail of fig. 244.

Plate 118.

246. Jan van Eyck; Detail of fig. 244.

Plate 119.

247. Jan van Eyck, Giovanni Arnolfini and Jeanne Cenami; London, National Gallery.

Plate 120.

248. Jan van Eyck, Madonna of Canon George van der Paele; Bruges, Musée Communal.

Plate 121.

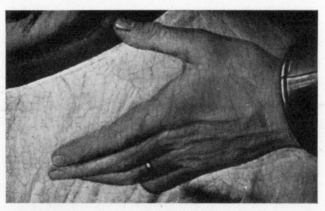

249. Jan van Eyck; Detail of fig. 248.

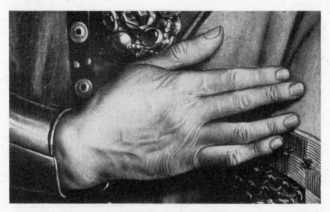

250. Master of Flémalle; Detail of fig. 205.

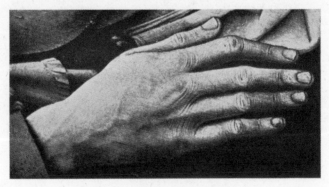

251. Roger van der Weyden; Detail of fig. 314.

Plate 122.

252. Jan van Eyck, the "Lucca Madonna"; Frankfort, Städelsches Kunstinstitut.

Plate 123.

253. Jan van Eyck, Annunciation; Lugano, Thyssen Coll.

Plate 124.

254. Jan van Eyck, St. Barbara; Antwerp, Musée Royal.

Plate 125.

255. Jan van Eyck, Madonna at the Fountain; Antwerp, Musée Royal.

Plate 126.

256. Jan van Eyck (?), The Holy Face; Durham, J. C. Swinborne Coll. (?).

Plate 127.

Plate 128.

258. Jan van Eyck and Petrus Christus, St. Jerome; Detroit, Institute of Arts.

Plate 129.

259. Commenced by Jan van Eyck, Triptych of Nicholas van Maelbeke; Ownership Not Established.

Plate 130.

260. Jan van Eyck, Baudouin de Lannoy; Berlin, Kaiser Friedrich Museum.

Plate 131.

261. Jan van Eyck, "Timotheos" (Gilles Binchois?); London, National Gallery.

Plate 132.

262. Jan van Eyck, Man in a Red Turban; London, National Gallery.

Plate 133.

263. Jan van Eyck, Nicholas Cardinal Albergati; Vienna, Gemäldegalerie.

Plate 134.

264. Jan van Eyck, Nicholas Cardinal Albergati (Silverpoint); Formerly Dresden, Kupferstichkabinett.

Plate 135.

265. Jan van Eyck, The Goldsmith Jan de Leeuw; Vienna, Gemäldegalerie.

Plate 136.

266. Jan van Eyck, Giovanni Arnolfini; Berlin, Kaiser Friedrich Museum.

Plate 137.

267. Jan van Eyck, Margaret van Eyck; Bruges, Musée Communal.

Plate 138.

268. Follower of Jan van Eyck, Stigmatization of St. Francis; Philadelphia,
Pennsylvania Museum of Art, Johnson Coll.

269. Follower of Jan van Eyck, Stigmatization of St. Francis;
Turin, Galleria Sabauda.

Plate 139.

271. Imitator of Jan van Eyck, The Man with the Pink; Berlin, Kaiser Friedrich Museum.

270. Imitator of Jan van Eyck, Portrait of a Goldsmith; Sibiu, Bruckenthal Museum.

Plate 140.

273. Unidentified Artist, St. George; Formerly London, Lady E. Mason Coll.

272. Pedro Nisart after Jan van Eyck, St. George; Palma, Museo Arqueológico.

Plate 141.

274. Jan van Eyck, Ghent Altarpiece, Exterior; Ghent, St. Bavo's.

Plate 142.

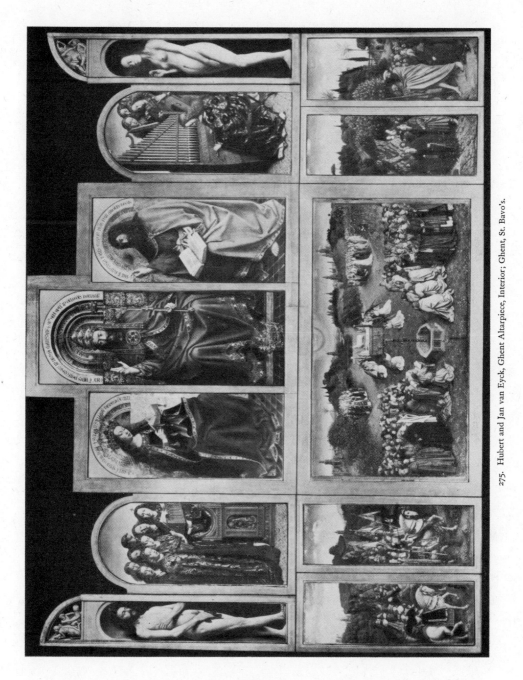

275. Hubert and Jan van Eyck, Ghent Altarpiece, Interior; Ghent, St. Bavo's.

Plate 143.

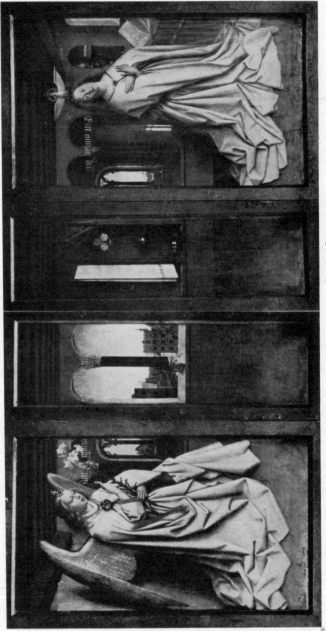

276. Jan van Eyck, Annunciation; Detail of fig. 274.

Plate 144.

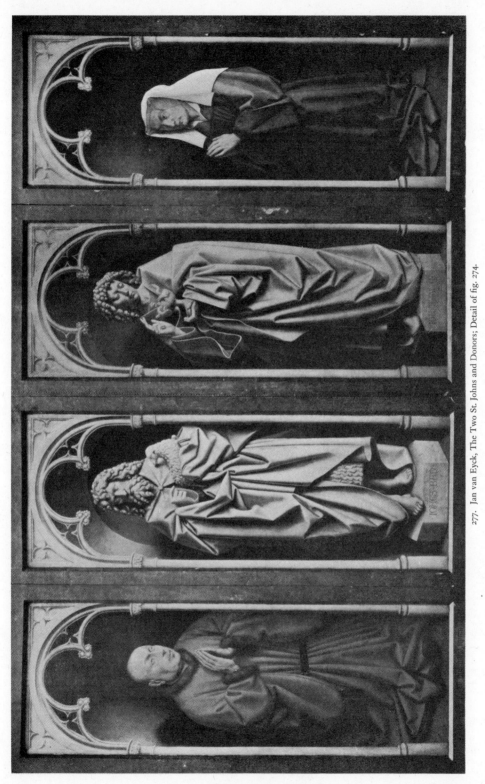

277. Jan van Eyck, The Two St. Johns and Donors; Detail of fig. 274.

Plate 145.

278. Hubert and Jan van Eyck, Adoration of the Lamb; Detail of fig. 275.

Plate 146.

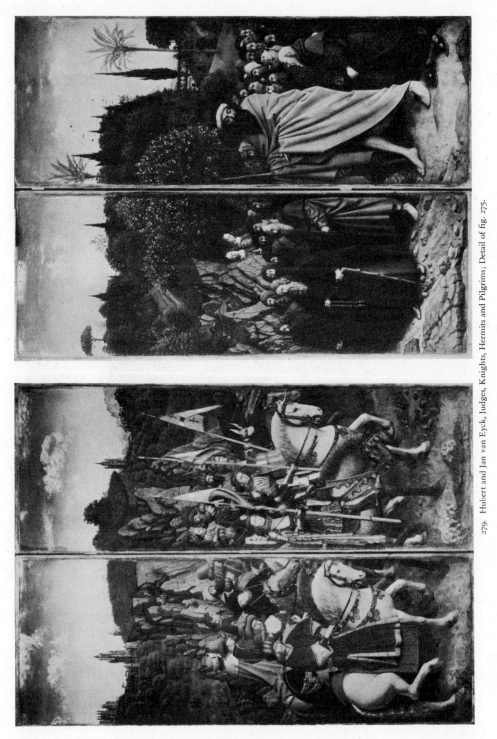

279. Hubert and Jan van Eyck, Judges, Knights, Hermits and Pilgrims; Detail of fig. 275.

Plate 147.

280. Hubert and Jan van Eyck, The Virgin Mary, The Lord, St. John the Baptist; Detail of fig. 275.

Plate 148.

281. Jan van Eyck, Adam and Eve; Detail of fig. 275.

Plate 149.

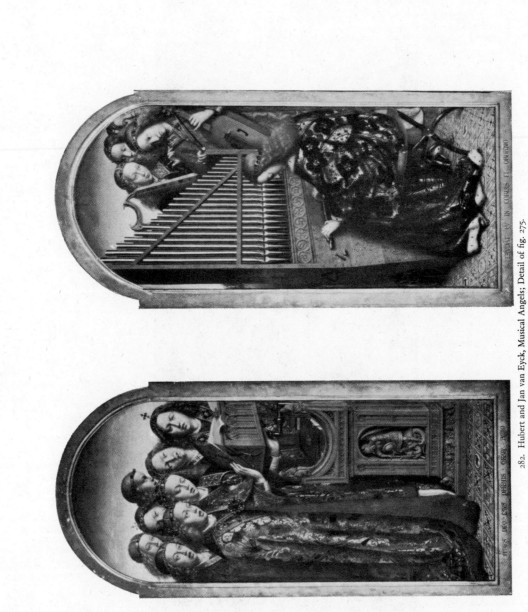

282. Hubert and Jan van Eyck, Musical Angels; Detail of fig. 275.

Plate 150.

283 a. Jan van Eyck, Virgin Martyrs; Detail of fig. 278.

283 b. Hubert van Eyck, Apostles; Detail of fig. 278.

Plate 151.

284. Hubert van Eyck (?), Annunciation; New York, Metropolitan Museum.

Plate 152.

285. Hubert and Jan van Eyck (?), The Three Marys at the Tomb; Vierhouten, van Beuningen Coll.

Plate 153.

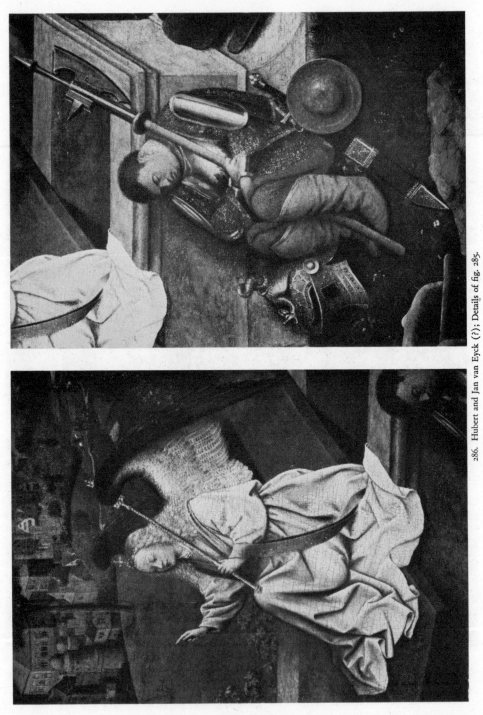

Plate 154.

288. Follower of Jan van Eyck, Agony in the Garden; Turin, Museo Civico, *Très-Belles Heures*.

287. Follower of Jan van Eyck, The Lord Enthroned; Formerly Turin, Royal Library, *Très-Belles Heures*.

Plate 155.

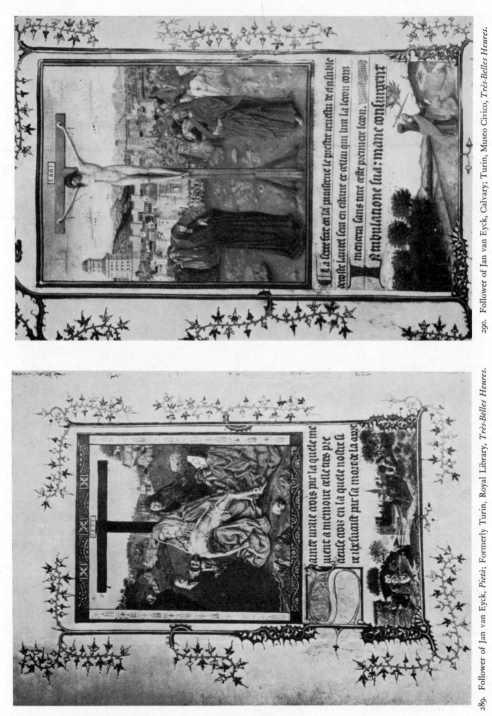

290. Follower of Jan van Eyck, Calvary; Turin, Museo Civico, *Très-Belles Heures.*

289. Follower of Jan van Eyck, *Pietà*; Formerly Turin, Royal Library, *Très-Belles Heures.*

Plate 156.

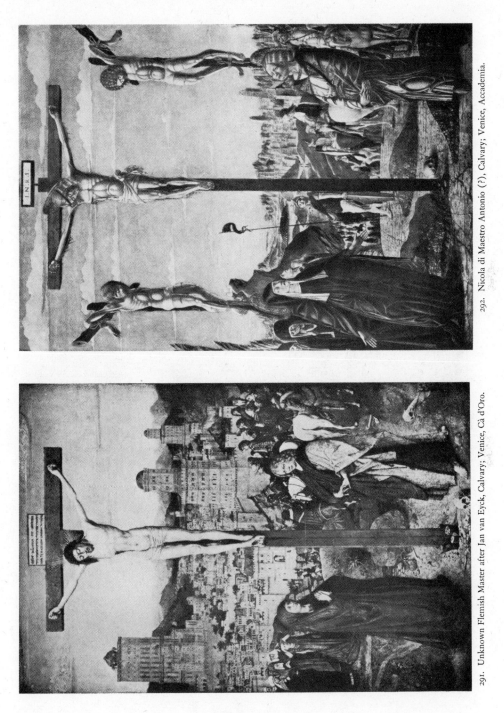

292. Nicola di Maestro Antonio (?), Calvary; Venice, Accademia.

291. Unknown Flemish Master after Jan van Eyck, Calvary; Venice, Cà d'Oro.

Plate 157.

293. Follower of Jan van Eyck, Crucifixion; Berlin, Kaiser Friedrich Museum.

Plate 158.

mnes sancte virgines mentis
et corporis puritatem.

294. Jan van Eyck, The Virgin Among Virgins; Formerly Turin, Royal Library, *Très-Belles Heures*.

Plate 159.

os autem gloriari oportet in cruce dñi
nostri iħesu xpristi in quo est salus uita
et resurrectio nostra per quem saluati +
liberati sumus. pš. ideus miseratur

295. Jan van Eyck, Finding of the True Cross; Turin, Museo Civico, *Très-Belles Heures*.

Plate 160.

296. Jan van Eyck, St. Julian Ferrying Christ; Formerly Turin, Royal Library, *Très-Belles Heures*.

Plate 161.

297. Jan van Eyck, Prayer on the Shore; Formerly Turin, Royal Library, *Très-Belles Heures*.

Plate 162.

298. Jan van Eyck, Betrayal of Christ; Formerly Turin, Royal Library, *Très-Belles Heures*.

Plate 163.

299. Jan van Eyck, Birth of St. John; Turin, Museo Civico, *Très-Belles Heures*.

Plate 164.

300. Jan van Eyck, Mass of the Dead; Turin, Museo Civico, *Très-Belles Heures.*

Plate 165.

301. Jan van Eyck, Diptych; New York, Metropolitan Museum.

Plate 166.

302. Copy after Jan van Eyck, Adoration of the Magi (Pen); Berlin, Kupferstichkabinett.

Plate 167.

303. Jan van Eyck, Details of fig. 301.

Plate 168.

304. Free Copy after Jan van Eyck, Bearing of the Cross (Pen); Vienna, Albertina.

305. Free Copy after Jan van Eyck, Bearing of the Cross; Budapest,
Museum of Fine Arts.

Plate 169.

306. Roger van der Weyden, Madonna Enthroned; Lugano, Thyssen Collection.

Plate 170.

308. Co-worker of Roger van der Weyden, St. Catherine; Vienna, Gemäldegalerie.

307. Roger van der Weyden, Madonna Standing; Vienna, Gemäldegalerie.

Plate 171.

309 a.

309 b.

309 c.

309. Roger van der Weyden and Follower, Triptych; Turin, Galleria Sabauda (a and c), and Paris, Louvre (b).

Plate 172.

310. Roger van der Weyden, Annunciation (Central Panel of fig. 309); Paris, Louvre.

Plate 173.

312. Follower of Roger van der Weyden, Visitation (fig. 309 c); Turin, Galleria Sabauda.

311. Roger van der Weyden, Visitation; Lützschena, Speck von Sternburg Coll.

Plate 174.

313. Roger van der Weyden (?), St. Luke Painting the Virgin; Boston, Museum of Fine Arts.

Plate 175.

314. Roger van der Weyden, Descent from the Cross; Madrid, Prado.

Plate 176.

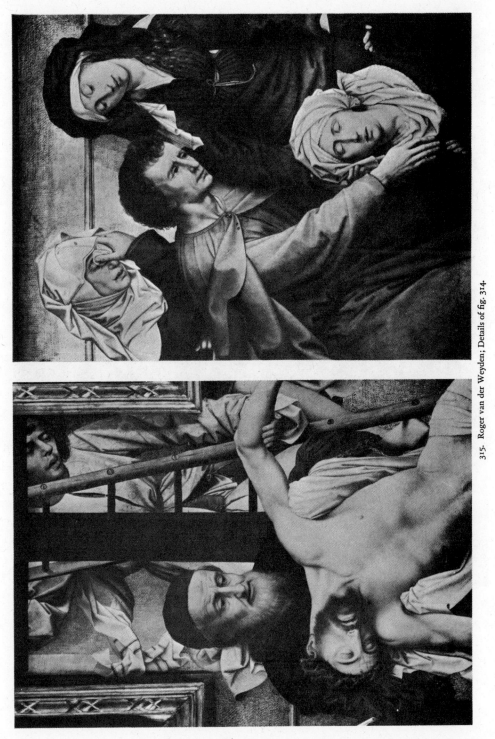

315. Roger van der Weyden; Details of fig. 314

Plate 177.

316. Roger van der Weyden, The Magdalen (Fragment); London, National Gallery.

Plate 178.

317. Roger van der Weyden, Madonna Enthroned; Madrid, Prado.

Plate 179.

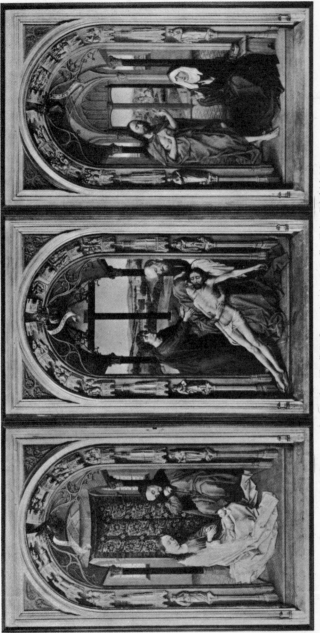

318. Roger van der Weyden, The "Miraflores Altarpiece"; Berlin, Kaiser Friedrich Museum.

Plate 180.

319. Roger van der Weyden, Holy Family; Left Panel of fig. 318.

Plate 181.

320. Roger van der Weyden, Lamentation; Central Panel of fig. 318.

Plate 182.

321. Roger van der Weyden, Christ Appearing to His Mother; New York, Metropolitan Museum.

Plate 183.

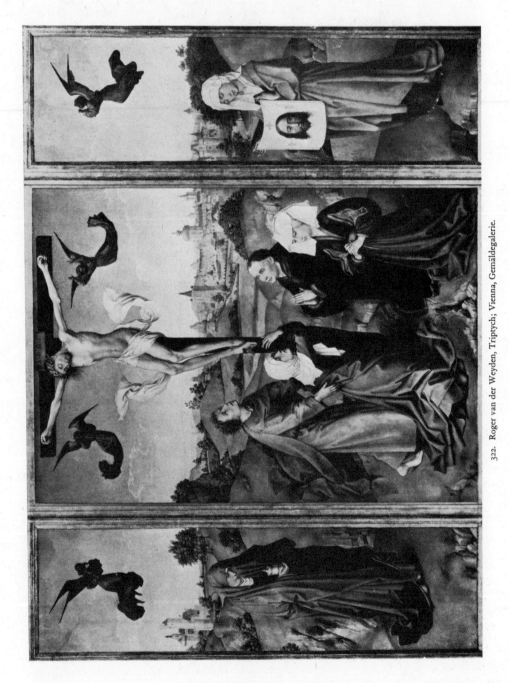

322. Roger van der Weyden, Triptych; Vienna, Gemäldegalerie.

Plate 184.

323. Roger van der Weyden; Detail of fig. 322.

Plate 185.

324. Roger van der Weyden; Detail of fig. 322.

Plate 186.

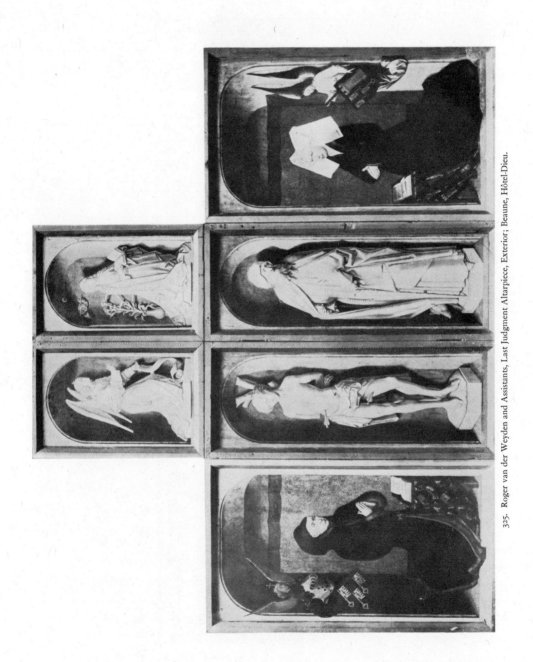

325. Roger van der Weyden and Assistants, Last Judgment Altarpiece, Exterior; Beaune, Hôtel-Dieu.

Plate 187.

326. Roger van der Weyden, Last Judgment Altarpiece, Interior; Beaune, Hôtel-Dieu.

Plate 188.

327. Roger van der Weyden, The Judge and St. Michael; Detail of fig. 326.

Plate 189.

328. Roger van der Weyden; Detail of fig. 326.

Plate 190.

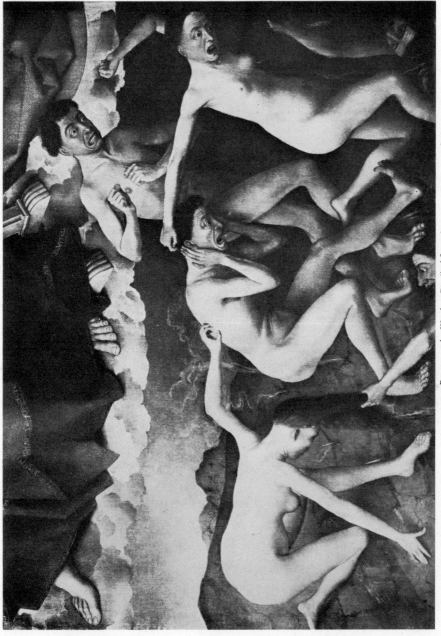

329. Roger van der Weyden; Detail of fig. 326.

Plate 191.

330. Dedication Page, Probably Designed by Roger van der Weyden; Brussels, Bib. Royale, ms. 941.

Plate 192.

331. Roger van der Weyden, Entombment; Florence, Uffizi.

Plate 193.

332. Roger van der Weyden, Madonna and Saints; Frankfort, Städelsches Kunstinstitut.

Plate 194.

333. Roger van der Weyden, Triptych of Jean de Braque; Paris, Louvre.

Plate 195.

334. Roger van der Weyden, The Magdalen; Right Wing of fig. 333.

Plate 196.

335·

336.

335, 336. Roger van der Weyden and Assistant, The "Bladelin Altarpiece"; Berlin, Kaiser Friedrich Museum.

Plate 197.

337. Roger van der Weyden, Nativity; Central Panel of fig. 336.

Plate 198.

338. Roger van der Weyden, The Visions of Augustus (a) and the Three Magi (b); Wings of fig. 336.

Plate 199.

339. Roger van der Weyden; Detail of fig. 337.

Plate 200.

341. Roger van der Weyden, David Receiving the Cistern Water (fragment):
Formerly Paris, Schloss Coll.

340. Roger van der Weyden, Augustus and the Sibyl of Tibur;
Detail of fig. 338.

Plate 201.

342. Roger van der Weyden, The St. John Altarpiece; Berlin, Kaiser Friedrich Museum.

Plate 202.

343. Roger van der Weyden, Birth and Naming of St. John the Baptist; Left Panel of fig. 342.

Plate 203.

344. Roger van der Weyden, Baptism of Christ; Central Panel of fig. 342.

Plate 204.

345. Roger van der Weyden, Martyrdom of St. John the Baptist; Right Panel of fig. 342.

Plate 205.

346. Roger van der Weyden; Detail of fig. 343.

Plate 206.

347. Roger van der Weyden (Executed by Assistant), Altarpiece of the Seven Sacraments; Antwerp, Mus. Royal.

Plate 207.

348. Roger van der Weyden (Executed by Assistant), The Eucharist;
Central Panel of fig. 347.

Plate 208.

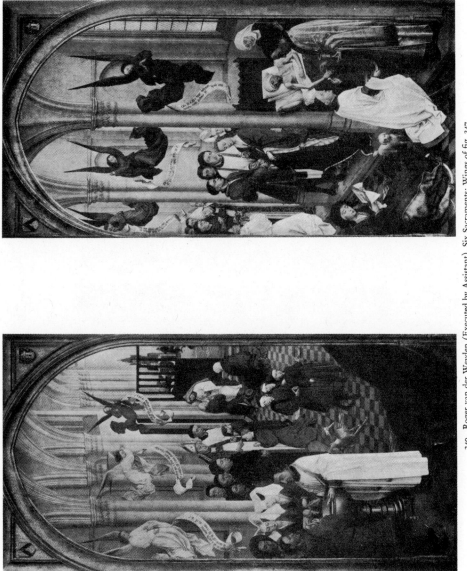

349. Roger van der Weyden (Executed by Assistant), Six Sacraments; Wings of fig. 347.

Plate 209.

350. Roger van der Weyden, Calvary, Left Wing; Philadelphia,
Pennsylvania Museum of Art, Johnson Coll.

Plate 210.

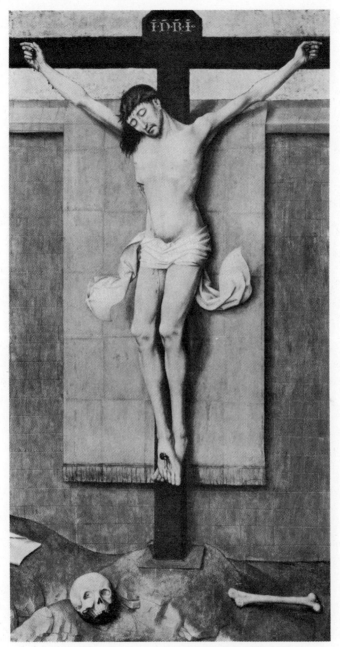

351. Roger van der Weyden, Calvary, Right Wing; Philadelphia,
Pennsylvania Museum of Art, Johnson Coll.

Plate 211.

352. Roger van der Weyden, The "Columba Altarpiece"; Munich, Alte Pinakothek.

Plate 212.

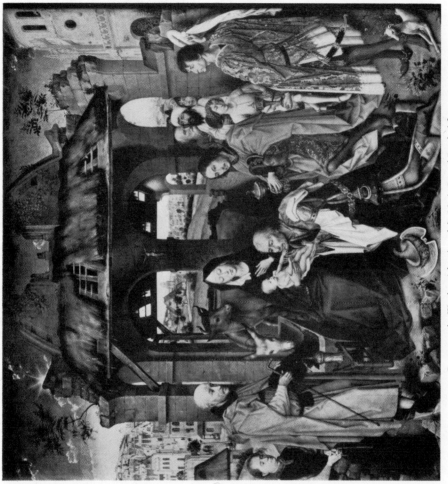

353. Roger van der Weyden, Adoration of the Magi; Central Panel of fig. 352.

Plate 213.

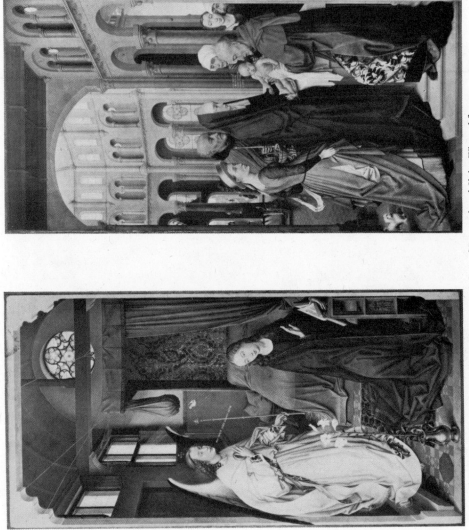

Plate 214.

355. Roger van der Weyden; Detail of fig. 353.

Plate 215.

356. Roger van der Weyden; Detail of fig. 353.

Plate 216.

357. Roger van der Weyden, Crucifixion; Escorial.

Plate 217.

358. Roger van der Weyden; Detail of fig. 357 before Restoration.

Plate 218.

359. Follower of Roger van der Weyden, Lamentation; The Hague, Mauritshuis.

Plate 219.

360. Roger van der Weyden, Portrait of a Young Lady; Berlin, Kaiser Friedrich Museum.

Plate 220.

361. Roger van der Weyden, Portrait of a Man in Prayer; New York, Metropolitan Museum.

362. Roger van der Weyden, Portrait of Guillaume Fillastre; Maidenhead, Sir Thomas Ralph Merton Coll.

Plate 221.

363. Roger van der Weyden, Isabella of Portugal Designated as the Persian Sibyl; New York, John D. Rockefeller, Jr., Coll.

Plate 222.

364. Roger van der Weyden, Portrait of a Gentleman; Lugano, Thyssen Coll.

Plate 223.

365. Roger van der Weyden, *The Grand Bâtard de Bourgogne*; Brussels, Mus. Royal.

Plate 224.

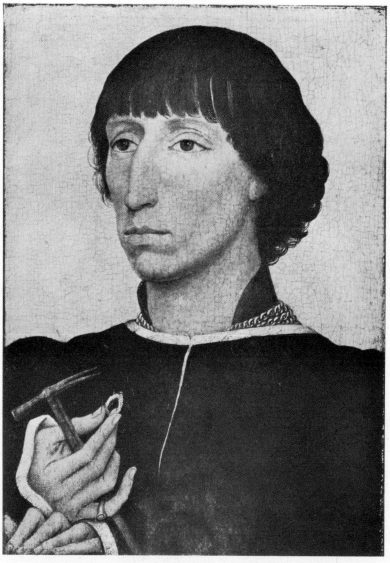

366. Roger van der Weyden, Francesco d'Este; New York, Metropolitan Museum.

Plate 225.

367. Roger van der Weyden, Portrait of a Young Lady; Washington, National Gallery.

Plate 226.

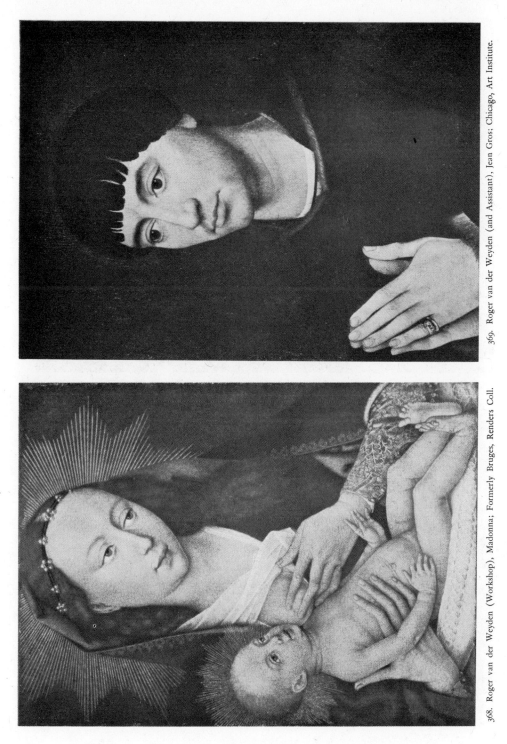

Plate 227.

Plate 228.

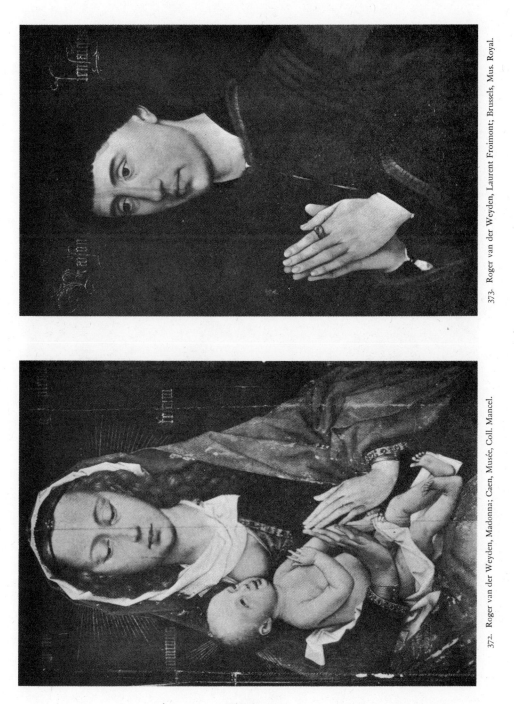

373. Roger van der Weyden, Laurent Froimont; Brussels, Mus. Royal.

372. Roger van der Weyden, Madonna; Caen, Musée, Coll. Mancel.

Plate 229.

374. Roger van der Weyden, Madonna; Donaueschingen, Galerie.

Plate 230.

375. Roger van der Weyden, Madonna (Replica); Houston, Museum of Fine Arts (Straus Coll.).

Plate 231.

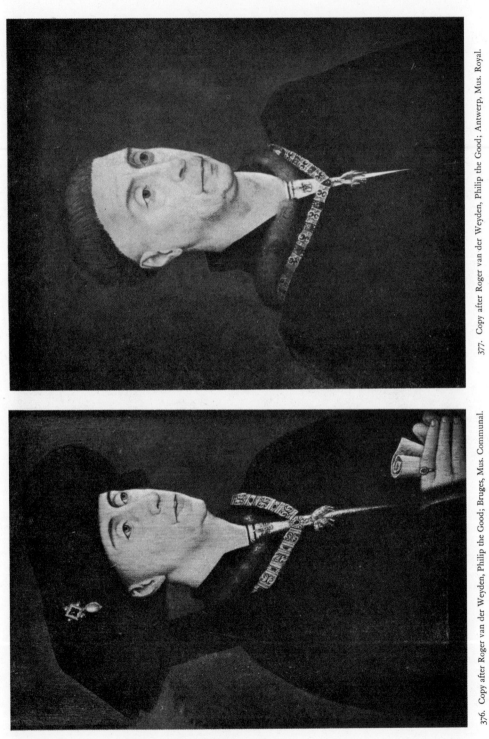

377. Copy after Roger van der Weyden, Philip the Good; Antwerp. Mus. Royal.

376. Copy after Roger van der Weyden, Philip the Good; Bruges, Mus. Communal.

Plate 232.

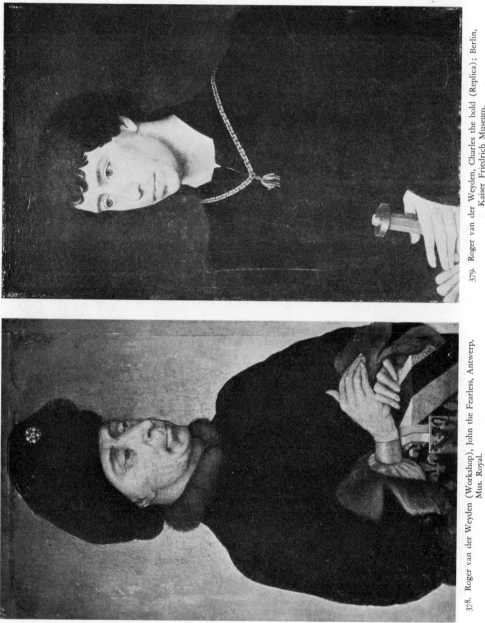

Plate 233.

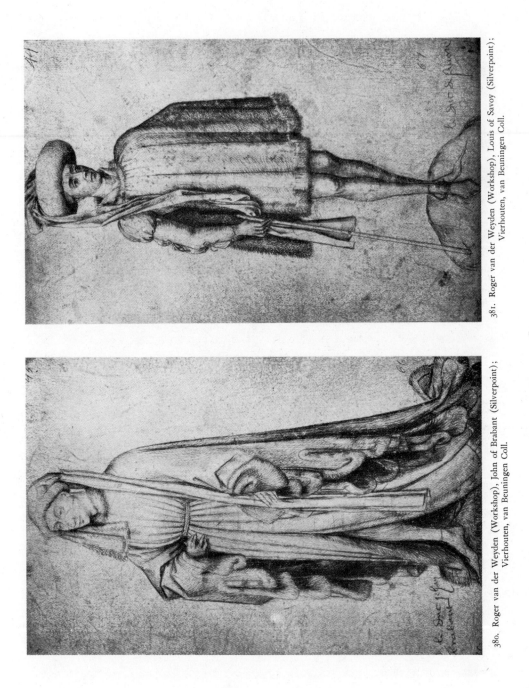

381. Roger van der Weyden (Workshop), Louis of Savoy (Silverpoint); Vierhouten, van Beuningen Coll.

380. Roger van der Weyden (Workshop), John of Brabant (Silverpoint); Vierhouten, van Beuningen Coll.

Plate 234.

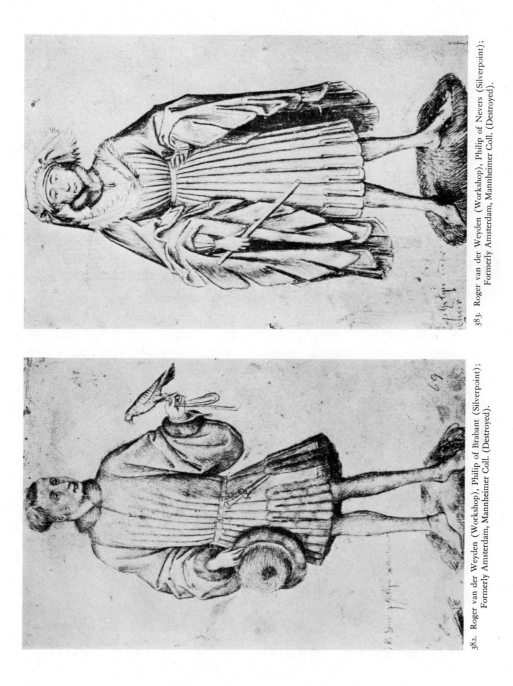

383. Roger van der Weyden (Workshop), Philip of Nevers (Silverpoint);
Formerly Amsterdam, Mannheimer Coll. (Destroyed).

382. Roger van der Weyden (Workshop), Philip of Brabant (Silverpoint);
Formerly Amsterdam, Mannheimer Coll. (Destroyed).

Plate 235.

384. Roger van der Weyden (?), The Magdalen (Silverpoint); London, Brit. Mus.

Plate 236.

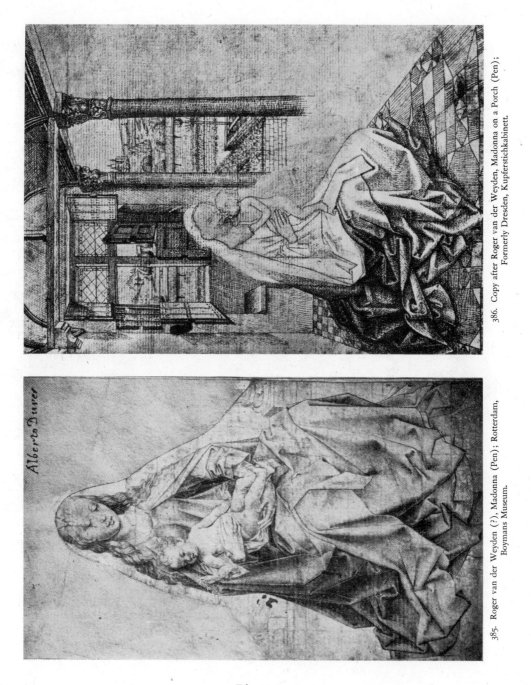

385. Roger van der Weyden (?), Madonna (Pen); Rotterdam, Boymans Museum.

386. Copy after Roger van der Weyden, Madonna on a Porch (Pen); Formerly Dresden, Kupferstichkabinett.

Plate 237.

387 a. Free Copy after Roger van der Weyden, Justice of Trajan and Herkinbald, Left Half (Tapestry); Berne, Historisches Museum.

Plate 238.

387 b. Free Copy after Roger van der Weyden, Justice of Trajan and Herkinbald, Right Half (Tapestry); Berne, Historisches Museum.

Plate 239.

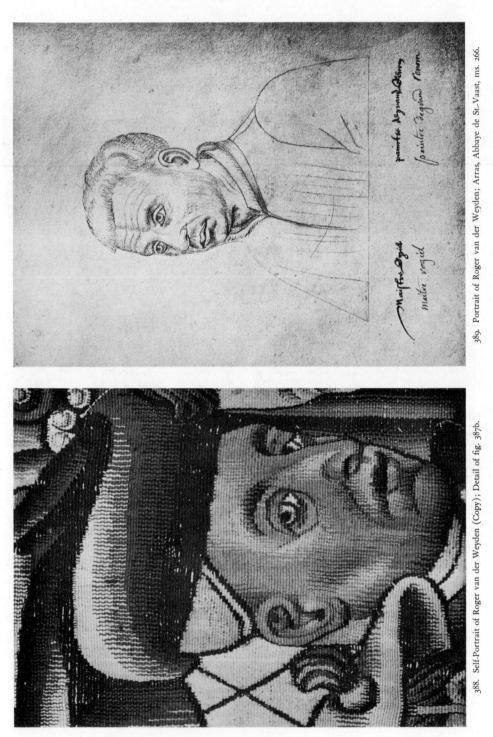

389. Portrait of Roger van der Weyden; Arras, Abbaye de St.-Vaast, ms. 266.

388. Self-Portrait of Roger van der Weyden (Copy); Detail of fig. 387b.

Plate 240.

390. Roger van der Weyden (Workshop), Lamentation; Brussels, Mus. Royal.

Plate 241.

392. Copy after Roger van der Weyden, Bearing of the Body to the
Sepulchre (Pen); Paris, Louvre.

391. Copy after Roger van der Weyden, Bearing of the
Cross (Pen); Formerly Leipzig, Prof. F. Becker.

Plate 242.

393. Copy after Roger van der Weyden (Vrancke van der Stockt?), Descent from the Cross; Munich, Alte Pinakothek.

Plate 243.

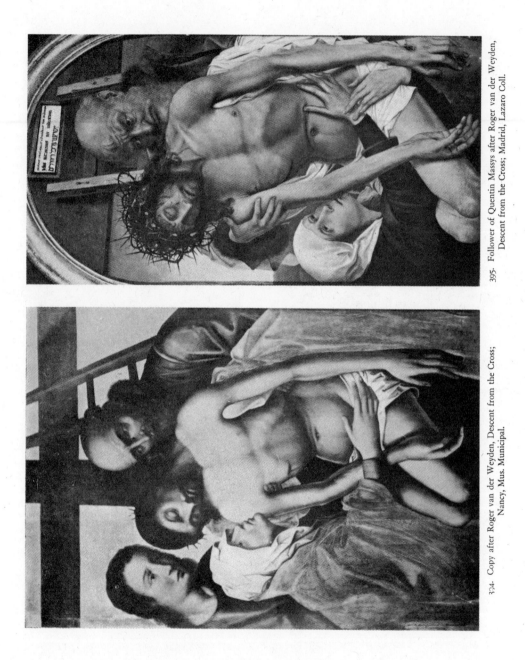

395. Follower of Quentin Massys after Roger van der Weyden,
Descent from the Cross; Madrid, Lazaro Coll.

394. Copy after Roger van der Weyden, Descent from the Cross;
Nancy, Mus. Municipal.

Plate 244.

397. Follower of Roger van der Weyden, Exhumation of St. Hubert; London, National Gallery.

396. Follower of Roger van der Weyden, Dream of Pope Sergius; Haartekamp, Mme. von Pannwitz Coll.

Plate 245.

398. Follower of Roger van der Weyden, Calvary; Berlin, Kaiser Friedrich Museum.

Plate 246.

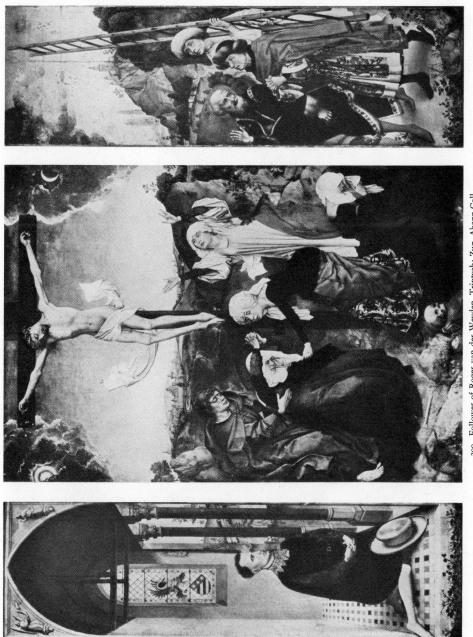

399. Follower of Roger van der Weyden, Triptych; Zug, Abegg Coll.

Plate 247.

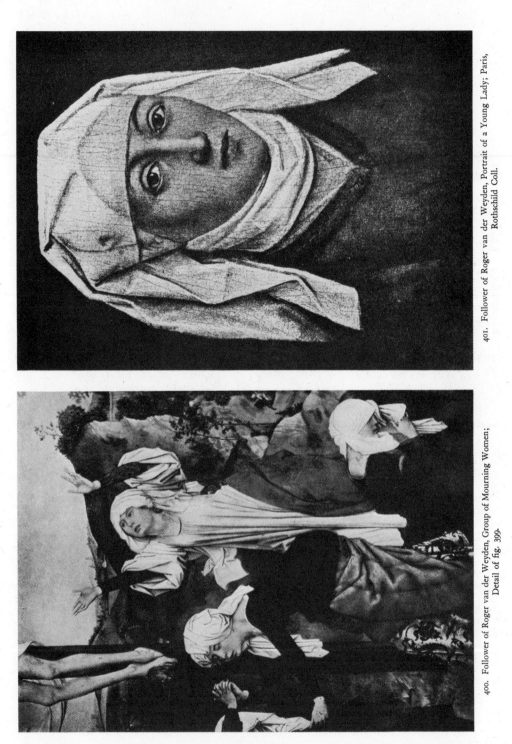

401. Follower of Roger van der Weyden, Portrait of a Young Lady; Paris, Rothschild Coll.

400. Follower of Roger van der Weyden, Group of Mourning Women; Detail of fig. 399.

Plate 248.

402. Petrus Christus, Nativity; Washington, National Gallery.

Plate 249.

403. Petrus Christus, Lamentation; Brussels, Mus. Royal.

Plate 250.

Plate 251.

405. Petrus Christus, Portrait of a Carthusian; New York, Metropolitan Museum.

Plate 252.

406. Petrus Christus, Edward Grymestone; Gorhambury, The Earl of Verulam (on loan to the National Gallery, London).

Plate 253.

407. Petrus Christus, St. Eloy; New York, Robert Lehman Coll.

Plate 254.

408. Petrus Christus, Madonna of Jan Vos ("Exeter Madonna"); Berlin, Kaiser Friedrich Museum.

Plate 255.

409. Petrus Christus, Annunciation and Nativity; Berlin,
Kaiser Friedrich Museum.

410. Petrus Christus, Last Judgment; Berlin,
Kaiser Friedrich Museum.

Plate 256.

411. Petrus Christus Nativity; New York, Mr. Georges Wildenstein (formerly H. Goldman Coll.).

Plate 257.

412. Petrus Christus, Madonna and Saints; Frankfort, Städelsches Kunstinstitut.

Plate 258.

413. Petrus Christus, Portrait of a Young Girl; Berlin, Kaiser Friedrich Museum.

Plate 259.

415. Dirc Bouts, Visitation; Madrid, Prado.

414. Dirc Bouts, Annunciation; Madrid, Prado.

Plate 260.

417. Dirc Bouts, Adoration of the Magi; Madrid, Prado.

416. Dirc Bouts, Nativity; Madrid, Prado.

Plate 261.

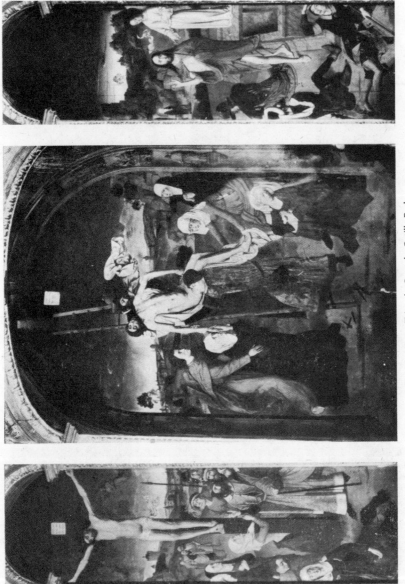

418. Dirc Bouts, Triptych; Granada, Capilla Real.

Plate 262.

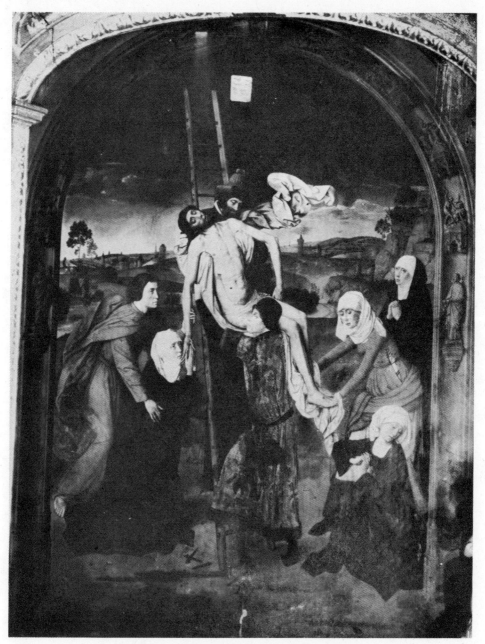

419. Dirc Bouts, Descent from the Cross; Central Panel of fig. 418.

Plate 263.

420. Dirc Bouts, Entombment; London, National Gallery.

Plate 264.

421. Dirc Bouts, Lamentation (Replica); Paris, Louvre.

Plate 265.

422. Dirc Bouts, Portrait of a Young Man; London, National Gallery.

Plate 266.

423. Follower of Dirc Bouts, Self-Portrait (Silverpoint); Northampton,
Smith College, Tryon Art Gall.

424. Copy after Petrus Christus, Portrait of a Falconer (Silverpoint); Frankfort,
Städelsches Kunstinstitut.

Plate 267.

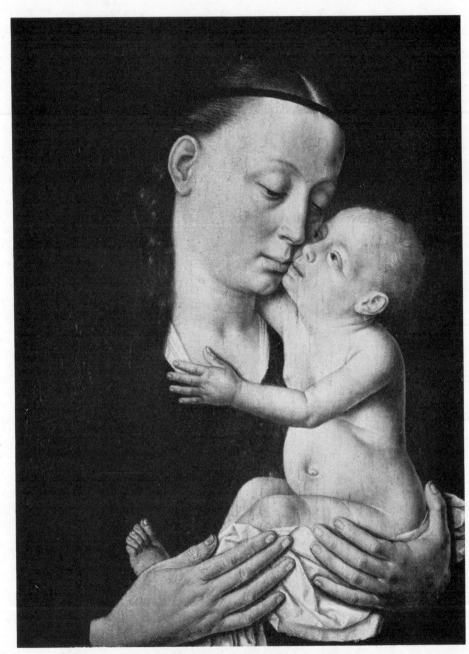

425. Dirc Bouts, Madonna; New York, Metropolitan Museum.

Plate 268.

426. Dirc Bouts, Madonna; London, National Gallery.

Plate 269.

427. Dirc Bouts, Triptych; Louvain, St. Peter's.

Plate 270.

428. Dirc Bouts, Last Supper; Central Panel of Fig. 427.

Plate 271.

429. Dirc Bouts, Elijah in the Desert; Upper Right (?) Wing of fig. 427.

Plate 272.

430. Dirc Bouts, Gathering of Manna; Lower Left (?) Wing of fig. 427.

Plate 273.

431. Dirc Bouts, Wrongful Execution of the Count; Brussels, Mus. Royal.

Plate 274.

432. Dirc Bouts, Ordeal of the Countess; Brussels, Mus. Royal.

Plate 275.

433. Follower of Dirc Bouts, Adoration of the Magi (cf. fig. 434); Munich, Alte Pinakothek.

Plate 276.

434. Follower of Dirc Bouts, St. John the Baptist and St. Christopher; Wings of fig. 433.

Plate 277.

435. Albert van Ouwater, Raising of Lazarus; Berlin, Kaiser Friedrich Museum.

Plate 278.

436. Albert van Ouwater; Detail of fig. 435.

Plate 279.

437. Utrecht Master of *ca.* 1460, Triptych; Utrecht, Centraal Museum.

Plate 280.

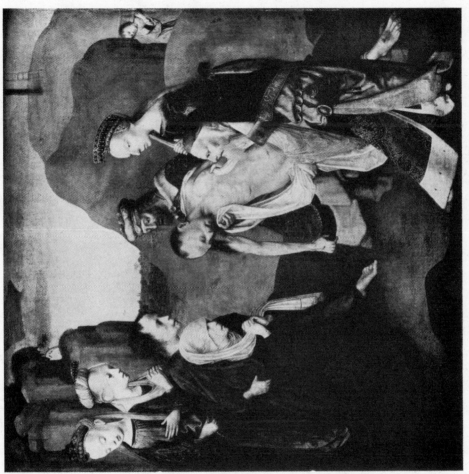

Plate 281.

439. Geertgen tot Sint Jans, Holy Kinship, Amsterdam, Rijksmuseum.

Plate 282.

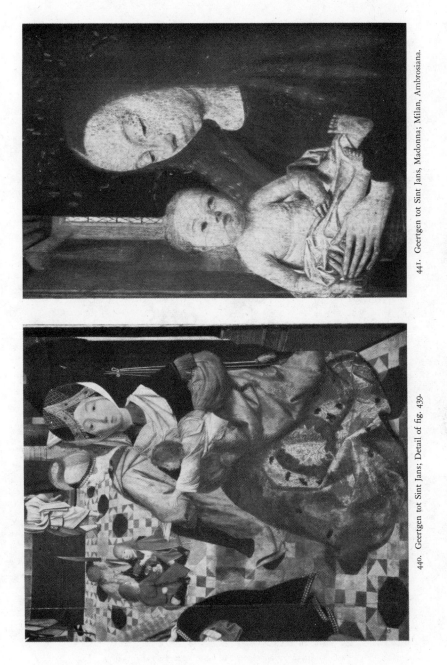

442. Geertgen tot Sint Jans, Raising of Lazarus; Paris, Louvre.

Plate 284.

443. Geertgen tot Sint Jans, St. John in the Wilderness; Berlin, Kaiser Friedrich Museum.

Plate 285.

444. Geertgen tot Sint Jans, Lamentation; Vienna, Gemäldegalerie.

Plate 286.

445. Geertgen tot Sint Jans, Story of the Remains of St. John the Baptist; Vienna, Gemäldegalerie.

Plate 287.

446. Geertgen tot Sint Jans; Detail of fig. 443.

Plate 288.

447. Geertgen tot Sint Jans, Madonna; Berlin, Kaiser Friedrich Museum.

Plate 289.

448. Geertgen tot Sint Jans, Nativity; London, National Gallery.

Plate 290.

449. Geertgen tot Sint Jans, Man of Sorrows; Utrecht, Archiepiscopal Museum

Plate 291.

450. Joos van Ghent, Adoration of the Magi; New York, Metropolitan Museum.

Plate 292.

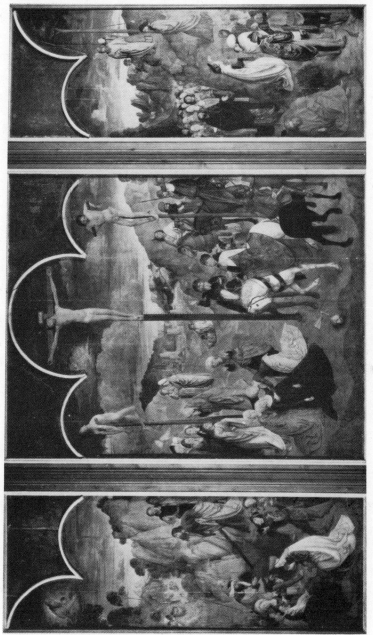

451. Joos van Ghent, Triptych; Ghent, St. Bavo's.

Plate 293.

452. Joos van Ghent, Calvary; Central Panel of fig. 451.

Plate 294.

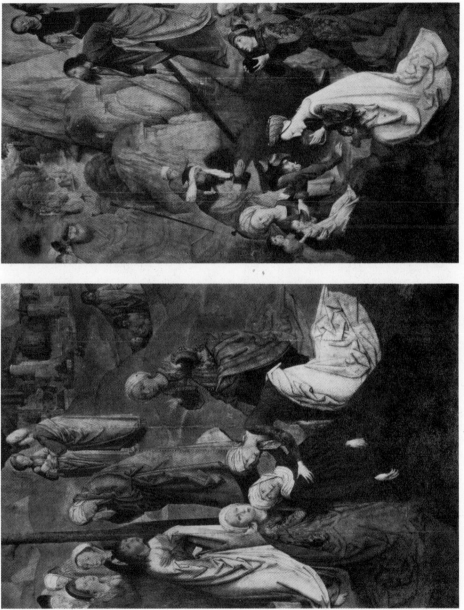

453. Joos van Ghent; Details of fig. 451.

Plate 295.

454. Joos van Ghent, Communion of the Apostles; Urbino, Palazzo Ducale.

Plate 296.

455. Hugo van der Goes and Follower, Triptych; Frankfort, Städelsches Kunstinstitut.

Plate 297.

456. Hugo van der Goes, Fall of Man; Vienna, Gemäldegalerie.

Plate 298.

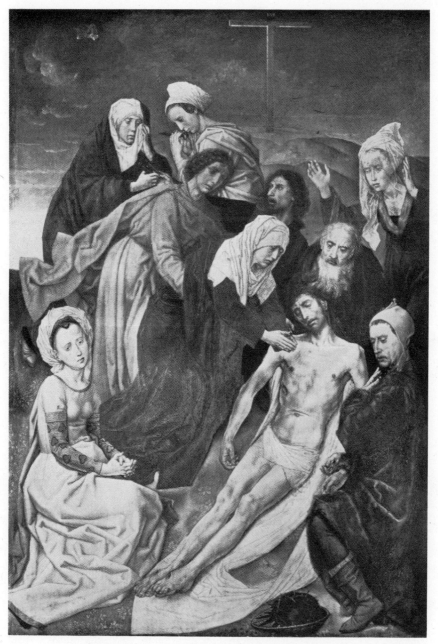

457. Hugo van der Goes, Lamentation; Vienna, Gemäldegalerie.

Plate 299.

458. Hugo van der Goes, St. Geneviève; Vienna, Gemäldegalerie.

Plate 300.

459. Hugo van der Goes, The "Monforte Altarpiece"; Berlin, Kaiser Friedrich Museum.

Plate 301.

460. Hugo van der Goes; Detail of fig. 459.

Plate 302.

461. Hugo van der Goes, The Portinari Altarpiece, Exterior; Florence, Uffizi.

Plate 303.

462. Hugo van der Goes, The Portinari Altarpiece, Interior; Florence, Uffizi.

Plate 304.

463. Hugo van der Goes, Nativity; Central Panel of fig. 462.

Plate 305.

464. Hugo van der Goes, Donors and Patron Saints; Wings of fig. 462.

Plate 306.

465. Hugo van der Goes, The Annunciate; Detail of fig. 461.

Plate 307.

466. Hugo van der Goes; Detail of fig. 464.

Plate 308.

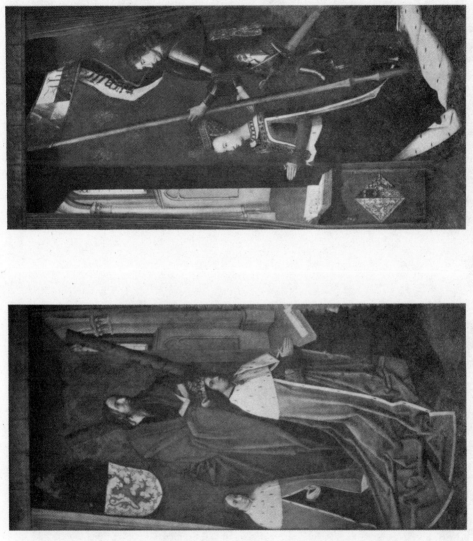

467. Hugo van der Goes and Followers, James III and Margaret of Scotland; Holyrood Palace
(on loan to the National Gallery of Scotland).

Plate 309.

468. Hugo van der Goes, Sir Edward Bonkil Venerating the Trinity; Holyrood Palace
(on loan to the National Gallery of Scotland).

Plate 310.

Plate 311.

471. Hugo van der Goes, Nativity; Berlin, Kaiser Friedrich Museum.

Plate 312.

472. Hugo van der Goes; Detail of fig. 471.

Plate 313.

473. Hugo van der Goes, Death of the Virgin; Bruges, Mus. Communal.

Plate 314.

474. Follower of Hugo van der Goes, Adoration of the Magi;
Vienna, Liechtenstein Gallery.

475. Follower of Hugo van der Goes, Nativity;
Wilton House, The Earl of Pembroke.

Plate 315.

476. Hans Memline, The Donne of Kidwelly Altarpiece; Chatsworth, Chatsworth Estates Company.

Plate 316.

477. Hans Memlinc, Portrait of a Young Fiancée; New York, Metropolitan Museum.

478. Hans Memlinc, Two Horses; Vierhouten, van Beuningen Coll.

Plate 317.

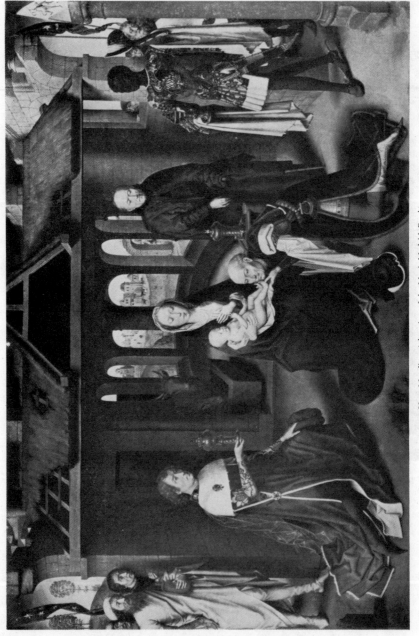

479. Hans Memlinc, Adoration of the Magi; Madrid, Prado.

Plate 318.

480. Hans Memlinc, Portrait of a Young Italian; Antwerp, Mus. Royal.

Plate 319.

481. Hans Memlinc, Madonna; Washington, National Gallery.

Plate 320.

482. Gerard David, The Lord Blessing; Paris, Louvre.

Plate 321.

483. Gerard David, Triptych; Paris, Louvre.

Plate 322.

484. Gerard David, The Virgin among Virgins; Rouen, Mus. de la Ville.

Plate 323.

485. Gerard David, Betrothal of St. Catherine; London, National Gallery.

Plate 324.

486. Gerard David, St. Catherine; Detail of fig. 485.

Plate 325.

487. Jan Gossart, Madonna in a Church; Rome, Galleria Doria.

Plate 326.

488. Jan Gossart, Deësis; Madrid, Prado.

Plate 327.

489. Quentin Massys, Madonna; Brussels, Mus. Royal.

Plate 328.

490. Quentin Massys, Madonna; London, Count A. Seilern Coll.

Plate 329.

491. Quentin Massys, The Money Changer and His Wife; Paris, Louvre.

Plate 330.

QVINTINVS
METSYS·PINGE·
BAT·ANNO·1513·

492. Quentin Massys, Portrait of an Elderly Man; Paris, Mus. Jacquemart-André.

Plate 331.

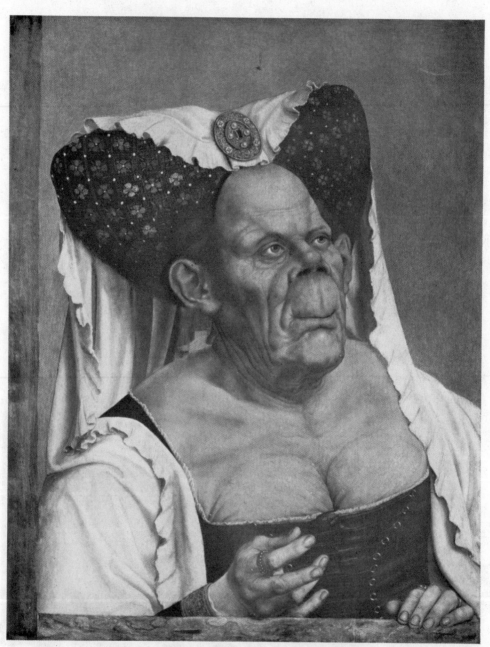

493. Quentin Massys, "The Ugly Duchess"; London, National Gallery.

Plate 332.

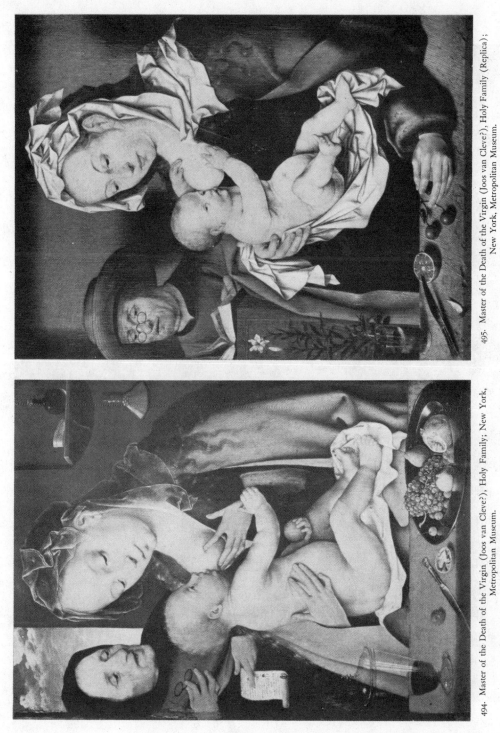

495. Master of the Death of the Virgin (Joos van Cleve?), Holy Family (Replica); New York, Metropolitan Museum.

494. Master of the Death of the Virgin (Joos van Cleve?), Holy Family; New York, Metropolitan Museum.

Plate 333.

496. Master of the Death of the Virgin (Joos van Cleve?), Holy Family; Lugano, Thyssen Coll.

Plate 334.